GW01117832

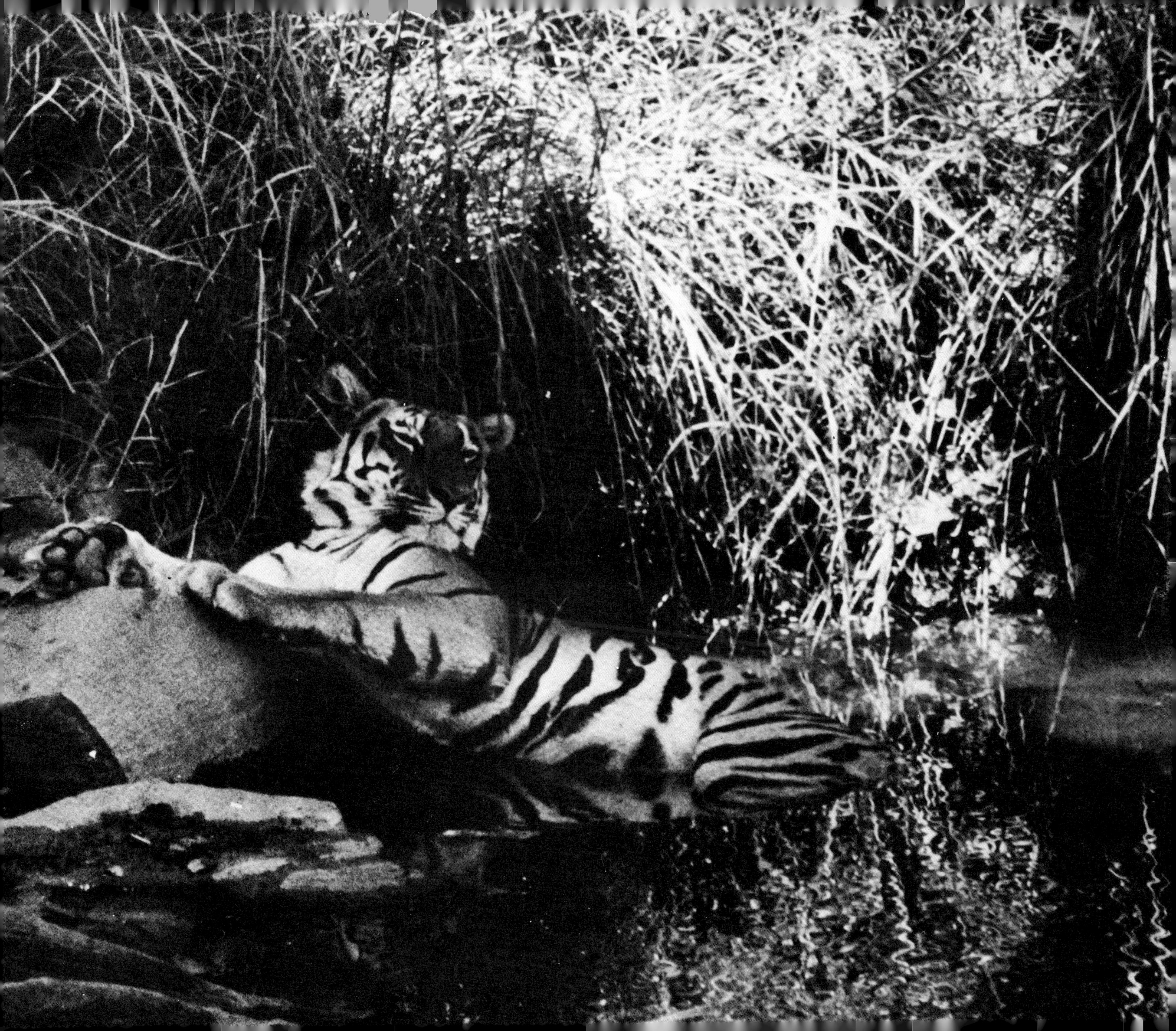

TIGERLAND

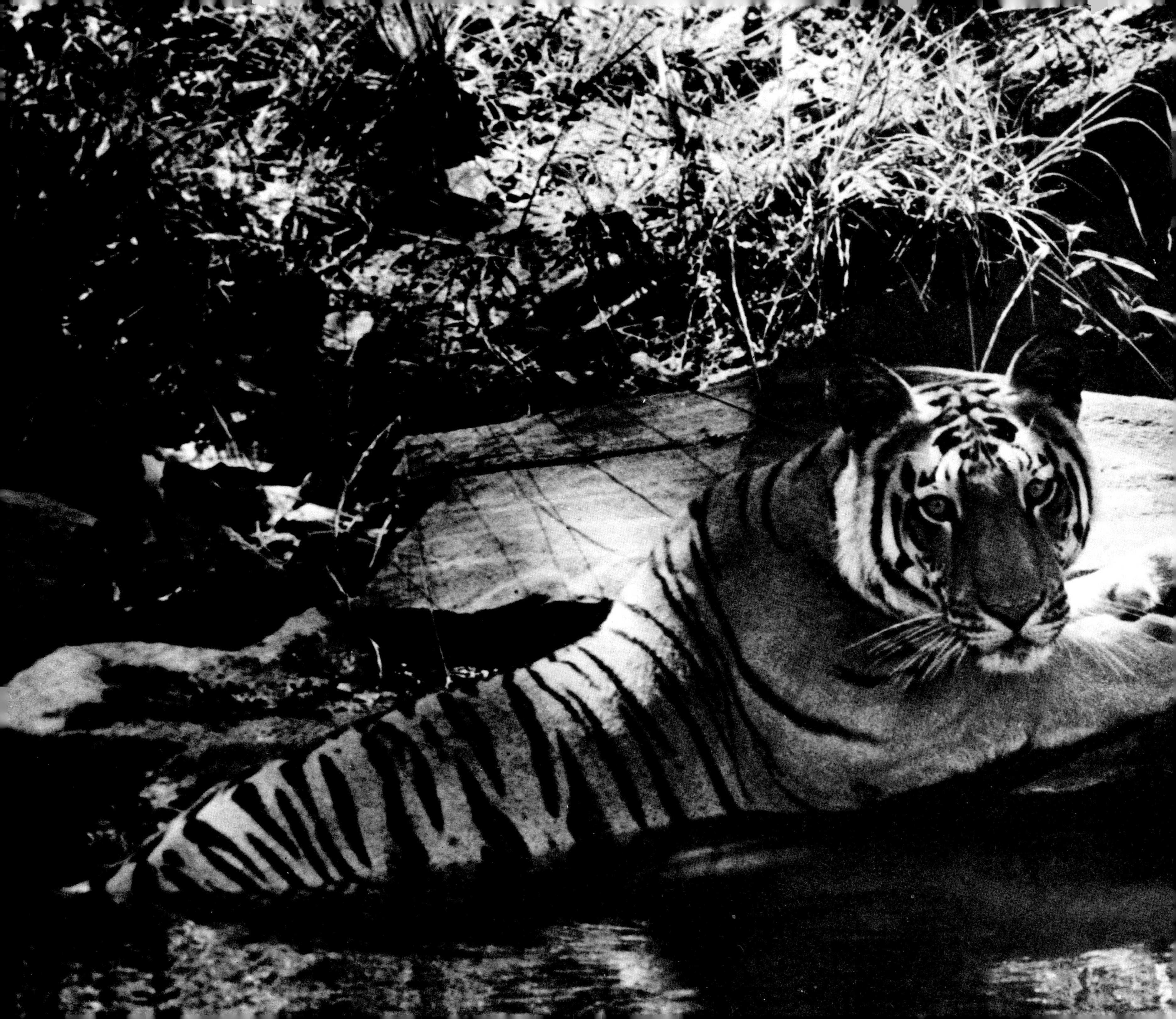

TIGERLAND

Kailash Sankhala

With a Foreword by Indira Gandhi

Collins

St James's Place, London · 1975

1 Bed-chamber *Endpaper*
It is rare for two tigers to live together except for a short period when courting and mating. They court the whole day long and mate as many as 54 times at an interval of 15–30 minutes. During the interval they sleep. These two I found sleeping, probably tired after a night's futile wandering. The click of my camera awoke the tigress, who looked at me and then returned to sleep.

2 PM's choice *Frontispiece*
During the summer, rivers and streams dry up, forming small pools. These remain the only source of water in the dry, deciduous forests. These river pools, especially the shaded ones, are the ideal place for the tigers to rest during the hot days. A partially submerged rock is cool and dry, and the tiger made no bid to leave even after he discovered my presence. This photograph was used by Mrs Gandhi as her 1973 greetings card.

Acknowledgements

It was Miss Padmaja Naidu and Dr Karan Singh of the Jawaharlal Nehru Memorial Fund who encouraged me to document the ecology of wildlife from the particular viewpoint of the Indian tiger. The Jawaharlal Nehru Memorial Fund freed me from a life of routine giving me unlimited opportunity to ramble in the wilds of India as well as a substantial grant to defray the expenses of wildlife photography. It was only with the help of Bernhard Grzimek of Frankfurt that I could get cameras and lenses of sufficient quality to take these photographs. A. R. Roy and N. N. Sen, my forester colleagues, have given me especial encouragement in my career, while G. K. Bora and Bharat Singh have helped me to plan my photographic expeditions. Game Wardens Fate Singh, Jaisingh, Rajasthan and Panney Singh have made my stays in their sanctuaries most rewarding. My son Pradeep assisted me in every aspect of my work. The project required long absences from home, and my wife Suraj has put up with all the inconveniences of living alone.

I am grateful to everyone for so much help.

Finally, a word about the Dedication of this book. I have a sad memory. While I was away studying tigers, my beloved daughter died. She had to wait for her last rites for four days until I came back from my field trip. She was my only daughter, and a stray thought haunts me still – that if I had not gone on my field trip her death would never have happened. Yet the will of God is supreme.

Foreword

No creature of the forests has captured the imagination of the Indian people as the tiger has done – except perhaps the elephant. The tiger motif dominates our folk song and folk painting. Now for the first time there is a danger that the tiger in its jungle might become a thing of memory. Progress and the search of a larger population for greater material satisfaction has led to encroachment of forests. The assault on wildlife began as a feudal sport. Economic pressure threatens to destroy it.

In India we have long thought of man as one of the species, without overriding rights on nature; but in practice he has been as grasping as men everywhere. People of all countries have at last begun to realize that man must not regard nature as a colony for him to exploit endlessly, and that the earth will support him only to the extent that he supports it. The extermination of species one by one is a warning and a threat to man himself.

An inborn love of animals and the wild was encouraged by my parents and enhanced by Kipling's jungle stories and later by Jim Corbett's entrancing description of tigers in the Kumaon Hills. The dull-skinned listless zoo animal gives no idea of what a magnificent creature the tiger is in his natural habitat.

Once, driving through a thickly wooded area in Karnataka, I was told by my hostess that, although there was a large variety of wild life, the season and the time of the day precluded our meeting any. Hardly had she ended her sentence when right in front of us I espied a tiger – the largest I have seen – stepping on to the road. Hearing the car, he paused to look us up and down. So did we. After a while he crossed over but squatted behind a bush by the roadside. We drove as softly as possible and stayed alongside to see more of him. I was lost in admiration of his grace and the controlled strength of the muscles rippling under his splendid coat. I would gladly have remained there, but the others were impatient of the delay and consequent disruption of the already tight schedule.

My next acquaintance with a tiger was even closer. We had three cubs, and one of them, whom we called 'Bhim', became exceedingly ill. I sat up nights to give him the prescribed

3 A birthday gift
An unusual present for the Prime Minister. The author presents Mrs Gandhi with a tiger cub on her birthday in 1968.

treatment. On the third day he lifted his head, and from then on we were good friends. He and the others stayed with us for several months until they grew quite big and a likely menace to the vast numbers of people who used to come to our house.

Not long after, my father was presented with a beautiful tiger skin and, for want of a better place, I kept it in our State sitting room. But every time I saw it I felt a pang at the thought of this proud king of the jungle being so humbled, and within a week I gave it to an American visitor.

It is indeed sad that lust for money and the desire of weak people to establish proof of their valour and strength are driving this superb species to extinction. We must do all we can to save the tiger. The Government of India, in co-operation with the World Wild Life Fund, has launched 'Project Tiger'. However, it is only the alertness of those who visit sanctuaries and the constant vigilance of every citizen wherever skins are sold, in spite of orders to the contrary, which can help to stop poaching and the trade in skins, and create the right public awareness of our fauna, a national heritage.

Shri Sankhala has portrayed the tiger in different moods. The book will render great service if, besides providing some moments of relaxation and pleasure, it succeeds in enthusing our people and enlisting their support to save the tiger for future generations.

New Delhi,
23 April, 1973

INDIRA GANDHI

Introduction

Over the last fifty years the number of tigers in India and throughout the world has decreased alarmingly. E. P. Gee, the famous Indian naturalist, estimated that at the turn of the century there were 40,000 tigers in India. This, however, was only an informed guess. A more reliable figure, based on calculating backwards from modern censuses, estimated that at the beginning of the Second World War there were 30,000 tigers. My own concern about the diminishing tiger population began in 1956, and to make out a case for its preservation I collected information from throughout India. My estimate, completed in 1969, was 2,500. As a result of this survey, the Indian government launched a massive 'operation census', and their final estimate, completed in 1971, came to 1,827. It would therefore be safe to put the total number of tigers in India, Nepal, Bhutan and Bangla Desh at around 2,000; but whatever the various margins of error it is clear that the tiger as a species is in jeopardy.

My own study showed that the foremost threat comes from cattle. Cattle compete with ungulates, which are the basic needs of tigers, for every blade of grass and every drop of water; they also drive the tiger into areas which are depleted of the resources tigers need and which are vulnerable to poachers. In addition, it is through cattle that various epidemic diseases are transmitted to the various prey populations of the tiger. Scant attention has been paid to this damage.

For an overpopulated country like India agricultural development is vital, and large-scale clearance of land plays an obvious part in this. However, wholesale destruction of tigerland in the Tarai region, both for agriculture and eucalyptus plantation, and the repeated burning of land for hill cultivation have ruined the best habitats of the tiger. Uncontrolled work on irrigation projects has further cleared extensive jungle areas and killed large numbers of animals, and not only the tiger. The dams have also submerged substantial areas formerly ideal for tigers. Further, in the major six tiger regions – the Assam Valley, the northern foothills and plains, the Western Peninsula, the Central Peninsula, the Western Ghats and the Sunderbans – the encroachments of civilization have led to many forest patches inhabited by tigers

4 Footprints of a tiger
These are known locally as 'pugmarks'. The last tiger census, conducted in 1972, was mainly based on the footprints of tigers. All information about size, sex, time of its departure and approximate mood of the animal can be inferred from the study of these pugmarks. In the recent past there were experts in the service of the Maharajas whose only function was to track and trace tigers with the help of pugmarks for 'sikar', or tiger hunts.

being cut off into small 'islands' of animal life. These 'islands' have no communication links or corridors, and therefore there are no chances of animal migration or gene exchange. On many, often only one or two tigers are to be found, and in such situations they are almost certainly doomed. The only remaining strongholds of tigers in India are now the Eastern Region, where there are some 456 tigers, and the Central Plateau, which has 800 tigers.

The misfortunes I have outlined so far have been due to man's carelessness. Far more ruthless have been the systematic attempts he has made to kill the tiger. Tribes living in the interior used to fit naturally into the ecology of the land, but with the increase in their population and with greater sophistication in the means of hunting this natural balance has been destroyed. Large-scale hunts, repeated month after month, have destroyed the habitat. Wildlife has been killed or even burned alive. Free licensing of arms, free trading in wildlife and its products and the lucrative incentives provided by such trade organizations as meat shops and fur emporiums have all played their part. Even zoos, who boast of their contribution to conservation, are guilty of killing tigresses and abducting the tiger cubs to build up their own stocks. Tourism, the so-called 'industry without smoke', consumed over 1,000 tigers in a short period of fifteen years by its much-advertised 'Tiger-Shikars', in which people were invited to destroy one of our magnificent beasts. Nor did these organized hunts end with killing tigers: those employed to beat out the tiger were paid not in cash but with a deer feast.

There is a long list of those who have shot 100 tigers, a feat many have performed a number of times. As recently as 1965 one Maharajah boasted of having personally shot 1150 tigers. The new monied class of contractors and traders have now become tiger hunters, eager to excel the record set by Jim Corbett, yet with no respect for life or law. But they too have been surpassed by the skin poachers, who poison tigers to get a hole-free skin. Before the ban on tiger hunting and the controls put on the trade in skins, the fur shops were full of tiger and leopard skins. Even after the ban, traders pleaded to be allowed to honour their pre-ban commitments – commitments which totalled over 2,000 tiger skins. If Dr Karan Singh, the Chairman of the Indian Board for Wild Life, had not reacted sharply against their proposal the tiger population would have disappeared.

Nor were government officials any more responsible. Travelling at government expense and without the need for permits, officials used their position to have tigers declared man-eaters, or at least as cattle-lifters. If tigers had lived in prides, like lions, rather than on their own, they would have been wiped out by now by the trophy hunters and fur traders, even before the ban.

There was no close period – unless it was for the benefit of the hunters, to save them from mosquitoes and drenching rains. High summer was the best period for the hunters; at a time when even birds kept their flying to a minimum because of the oppressive heat, tigers were driven over burning rocks to provide an easy target from a safe tree top or a well-built pillbox. No allowance was made for sex or age: many a tigress in an advanced state of pregnancy or with

DISTRIBUTION OF TIGERS

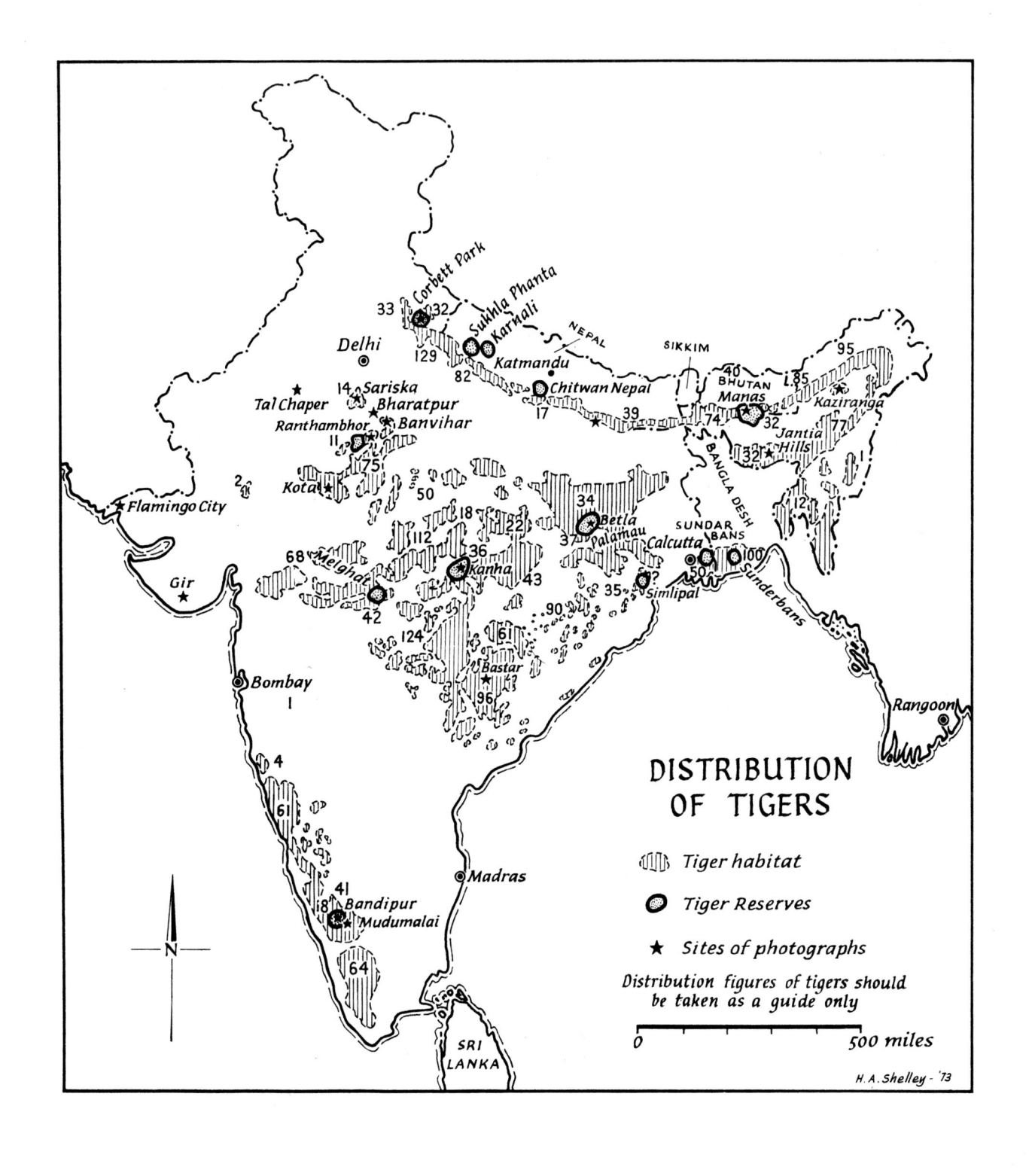

Legend:
- Tiger habitat
- Tiger Reserves
- ★ Sites of photographs

Distribution figures of tigers should be taken as a guide only

0 — 500 miles

H.A. Shelley - '73

5 On duty
With my camera in a typical part of Tigerland.

young cubs was killed.

These were the conditions until very recently – a virtual war on the tiger population. My lone voice pleading to save the tiger – or at least to spare him during the hottest period of the year – was drowned by the voices of the 'sportsmen'. My next attempt to get a ban on tiger hunting was voted down by the 'conservationists' in the Indian Board for Wild Life. The same year, based on information I had collected, the International Union for Conservation of Nature and Natural Resources included the Indian Tiger in its Red Data Book, and proposed a moratorium on tiger hunting. Luckily, India became the first country to accept the recommendation. Mrs Indira Gandhi wrote personally to her colleagues to help save the tiger, and later founded 'Project Tiger', a special attempt to protect the tiger and its lands. India is now to concentrate on eight special tiger reserves, each big enough to support a permanent and independent tiger population. Mrs Gandhi has allocated four million dollars to the project, and similar projects have now been started in Nepal, Bhutan and Bangla Desh. The world too has responded favourably, and the World Wildlife Fund has promised a further million dollars.

'Project Tiger' extends beyond simply the preservation of tigers in India: it takes in the need to preserve the whole of tigerland. For the tiger is at the apex of the biome pyramid of the land in which he lives, and every life form in his territory is influenced by his presence or absence. The tiger is a predator known ecologically as a 'second stage of consumer', one which needs primary consumers to prey on. Therefore to preserve and maintain the tiger a whole eco-system of producers and consumers has also to be preserved and maintained at a natural level. The tiger is exceptionally sensitive to any change in the environment. He will not stay to eat the last dead deer, but will leave an area well before the changes in his environment are clearly visible. He is the index of environmental quality.

The pictures in this book are thus of tigers, the land of tigers and the associates of tigers. Tigers live in close association with their prey – deer, antelopes, wild boars, wild buffaloes, gaur, even rhinoceros and elephants. Monkeys, lapwings and peafowls are their informers. Jackals, hyaenas and vultures are their camp followers, scavenging the left-overs. Leopards, and even men, share their domain as co-predators.

Ecological setting, behaviour display and other natural history aspects of wildlife, together with the quality of the picture, were the main considerations when selecting photographs for this book. But I would never select a photograph unless it represented the creature in its true state. The arrangement of the photographs does not always follow a particular order, and no attempt has been made to include examples of all Indian wildlife. If this book inspires a young naturalist to spend time in the Indian wilderness with his cameras and complete the task I have begun, I shall have the satisfaction of having contributed my modest share to the cause. I am sure someone will do it, and do it better.

6 My hides
Hides such as these blend well with their surroundings and if set up some time before an actual camera session are readily accepted by local wildlife.

Equipment

The photographs in this book were taken with two cameras – a big format 6 × 6 cms Pratisix – with its interchangeable normal Biotar f.2.8, 180 mm Sonnar Carl Zeiss jena and a 500 mm f/5.6 Meyer Orestegor lens lent to me by Bernhard Grzimek of Frankfurt – and a 135 mm miniature camera Ashai Pentax SP 11 with a set of f.1.8 normal tekumar lenses, a 135 mm f/3.5 Soligar and a 300 mm f.4 automatic Pentax tekumar telephoto lens. I used an adapter to take both the telephoto lenses of the Pratisix on the miniature camera.

The choice of film was important. I used fast films of 400 ASA to cope with changes from light to shade; to obtain shadow details when light entering from sparse openings in thick foliage created a patchy effect; and also to record fast movement. In open landscape and during bright summer months I preferred a slow film of 50 or even 30 ASA. Length of film was another important consideration. I mostly used 30 exposure films for the miniature camera.

As field photography is subjected to hazards both in the field and in the laboratory, excessive use of raw film is the only answer. Sometimes, when the situation was extraordinary, I not only took extra snaps with varying shutter speeds and apertures but also took care to spill over a few snaps on more than one film. These films I processed at different intervals to avoid the risk of total loss through an accident in the laboratory.

Hides

I always made hides in advance, so that the change in the environment was accepted by local wildlife as part of the natural landscape. The type of hide depended on the situation. In open, flat country like the dry beds of ponds or the saline flat lands of the Rann I used an underground bunker with fox-holes to peep through. Sometimes the position gave excellent low-angle shots against the blue sky. In forest areas and open grasslands, brushwood and thatched grass hides were ideal. In rocky areas and stony riverbeds, a dry, random rubblestone structure with green thatching merged well with the background. After one or two cautious looks the animals would accept it without concern. A portable canvass hide was equally handy, but uncomfortable during the hot season. Animals do not easily see objects in the shade when they are standing in the light, so hides are best made under the shade of trees and bushes.

Once I was positioned in any hide, I was largely self-sufficient. Requirements were kept to a minimum. I preferred a reasonably comfortable hide with soft-foamed rubber cushions and extra pillows. In the tropical forests, especially near water on marshy spots, mosquitoes, flies and even cobras and other snakes were a great nuisance. I never took anything to read with me, as it would have resulted in the loss of valuable opportunities. I also built a 'machan' – a temporary shelter – in the forked branch of a tree. Since animals least expect danger from trees, they do not look up, and they rarely discovered my presence unless I made my movements obvious or climbed the tree when they were looking.

7 My watchtower
A perfect vantage point for observing life in and around the lake.

Stalking

I found a jeep to be the most versatile vehicle in open forests and scrublands, as well as where cart tracks exist, especially in Sariska, Ranthambhor, Hanha, Palamau and Bandipur sanctuaries. Driving helped me to cover long distances and to cruise around large areas in the shortest possible time. It was a great relief from tiring elephant rides, and more convenient than stalking on foot. The animals got used to inanimate transport much more quickly, and soon learned to ignore it completely. If I allowed the jeep to roll with the engine switched off it scared the animals – probably they took the 'silent roller' to be some unknown animal moving towards them.

Seasons to Photograph

Summer in India is very hot, and animals of the plains do not like the heat. This provides an excellent opportunity to photograph animals at waterholes. With the onset of the monsoon in late June or early July the whole landscape changes. The dry, drab vegetation is transformed into luscious green, and the open meadows fill with grazing herds. However, varying light conditions and the many insects do not make it the easiest time for taking photographs.

The season from October to early December, even in the meadows of Kanha, proved disappointing, as there is little activity and one is hampered by the tall grass and thick cover. Chital, which were seen in hundreds in other seasons, were only in small hind parties – a few mothers with fawns just born and others waiting to give birth. The cold season proved to be the best for photographing barasingha (*Cervus duvouceli branderi*) at Kanha Park, and sambar and nilgai courting in Ranthambhor and Sariska. The fights for possession of a hind or a nilgai in heat were the subject of special interest. Some animals like tigers and leopards and even jackals were found in fine coat. Sometimes a stag with full grown antlers in velvet seen in the early morning against the light provided excellent photographs.

Spring brought activity in chital herds, and the burnt pastures became green once again. Nature was again at her best, and once again a feast for a photo-naturalist. In my experience the ideal photographic season is from February to April, when the weather is more stable, the visibility better and waterholes are fewer.

Mornings and afternoons provide excellent light. I preferred morning light, especially for back-lighted subjects, but animals do not follow any hard and fast rule. Many of the photographs of sambar, chital, nilgai, wild boars, jackals and even tigers were taken when I least expected them during the hottest part of the day when the sun was overhead.

I always went alone on my photographic trips, partially for selfish reasons – I wanted exclusive photographs – but mostly to avoid a feeling of guilt when a full day spent in a hide resulted in a good friend seeing nothing of interest. Personally I do not recommend anybody to go in the company of another photographer-naturalist anywhere!

KAILASH SANKHALA

8 Measured steps
Having seen a possible target, this tigress lowered her head, bent her body and approached my flimsy grass hide. She got so close I was genuinely in great danger. However, finding only a metallic lens, she changed her mind.

9 Watching and waiting *Overleaf*
This tiger was not quite sure what to make of me and kept a close watch on everything I did.

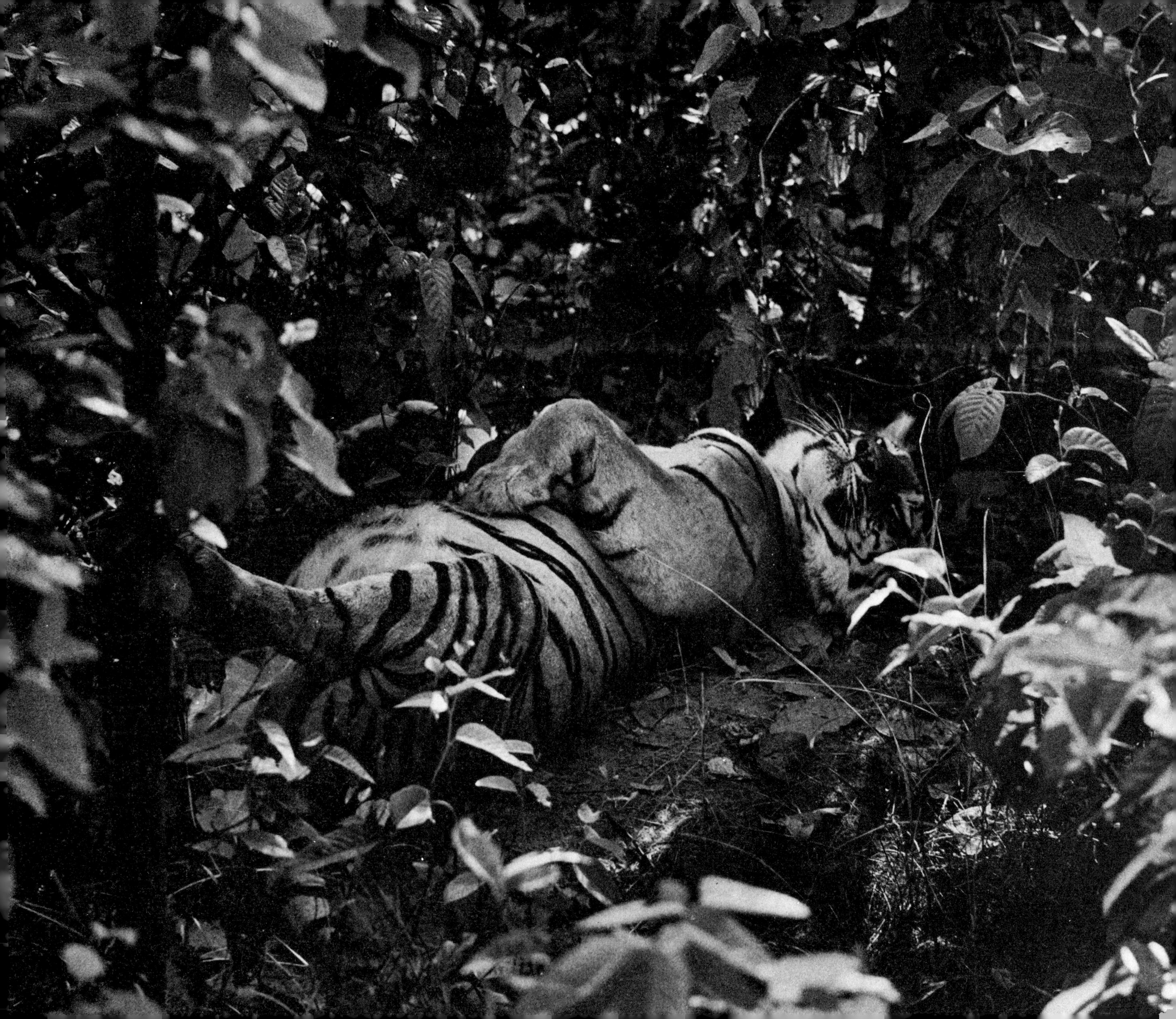

10 Pregnant tigress
A dry twig snapped under my feet and this alerted her. She turned her head, looked at me with half-open eyes and then ignored me.

11 Perambulator
It doesn't look very comfortable, but the cub is perfectly happy and co-operates with his mother by drawing in his legs and not moving. She carries the cub by holding his head between her canines. It is entirely her choice what pressure she exerts and how widely she opens her jaws, but there is no doubting the great love she has for her cubs.

12 **Quiet cover**
Tigers love to find a cool place where they can retire in the heat of the day. This tigress was disturbed by my sudden approach, looked into my eyes, snarled and left.

13 **On the rock**
Tigers enjoy shaded rocks, as they are cool in the morning. The position allows him to know of any approaching intruder in advance to plan an escape – or an attack.

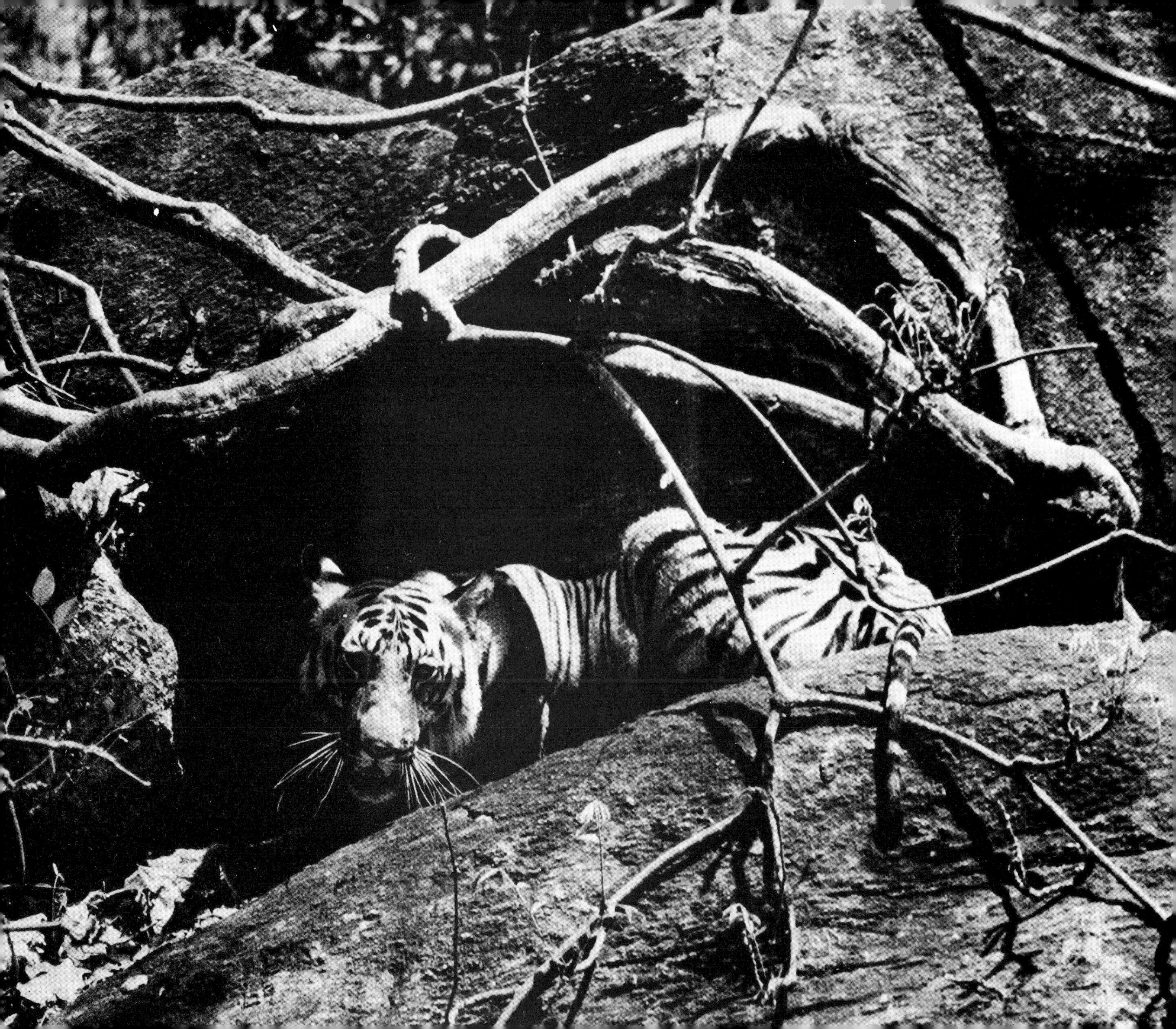

14 Ambush
A tigress conceals herself in an open patch of short grass, at the same time keeping her prey in sight so she can make a surprise attack at the most opportune moment.

15 Morning Walk
The reward of a long wait in the hide was this low-angle photograph. The tiger was coming to his natural kill rather too early. His attention was attracted by my presence in the hide.

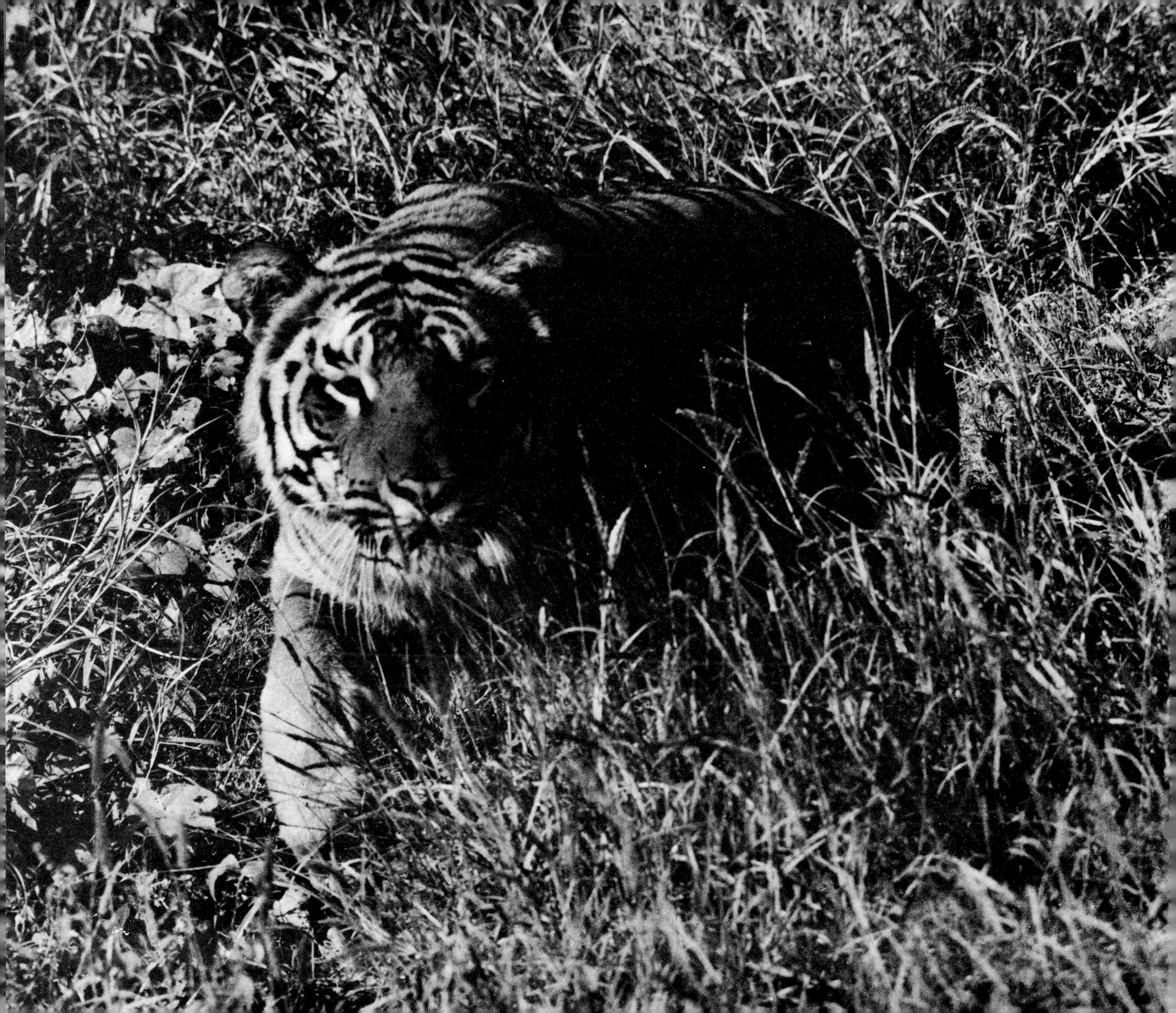

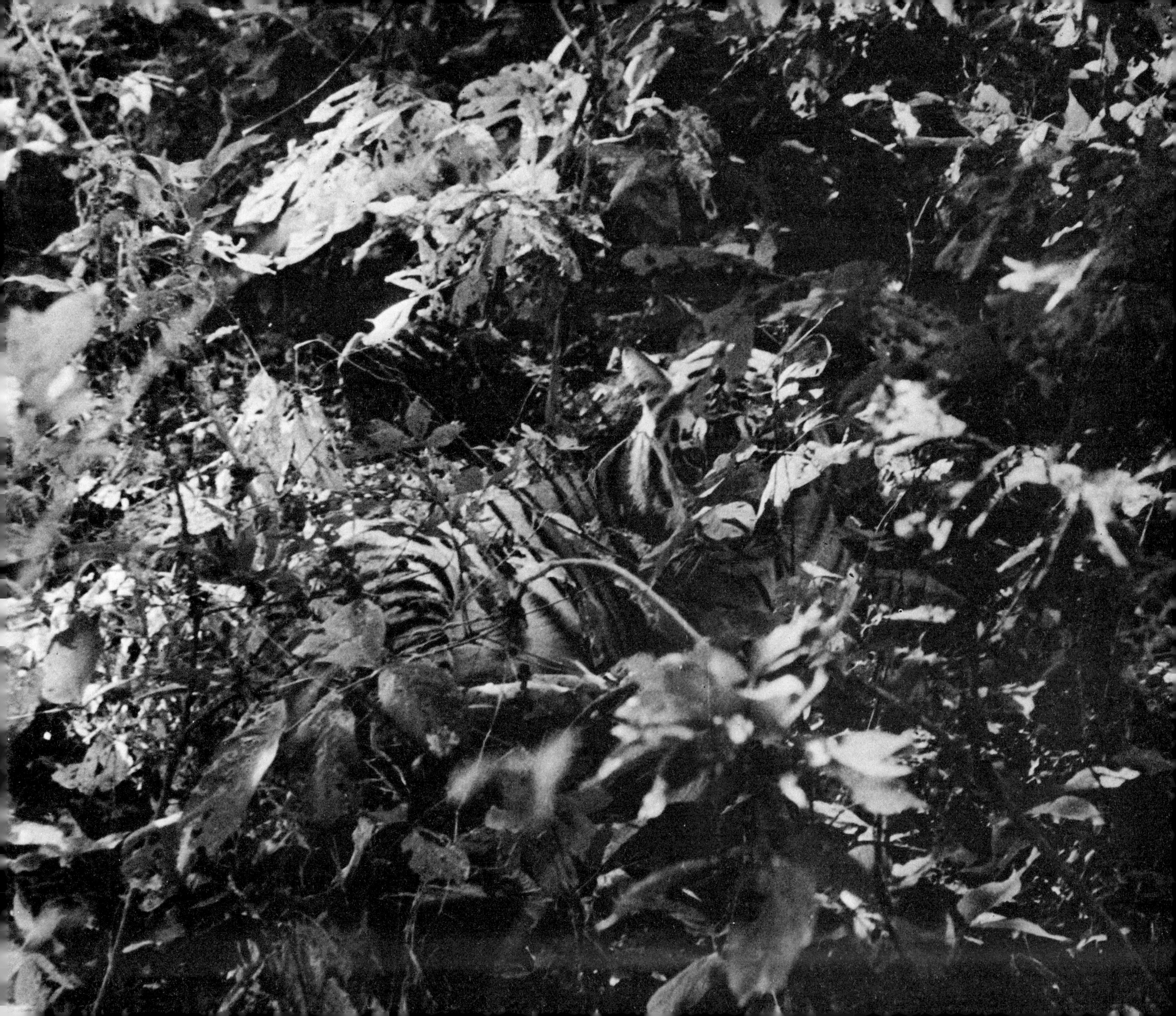

18 Trace the tiger
The bright colour of the tiger merges with the yellow of the drying foliage and the black stripes with the shadows of burnt vegetation. The camouflage is so perfect that, even if you are able to spot the tiger, a slight change of position and you can lose him again.

19 Look-out post
He knows nobody can trace him. Here, well in the shade and on a rock overlooking a river, he has a perfect vantage point from which to watch for game as it comes to drink water.

20 A mother acts as a decoy
　　Tigers never expose themselves unnecessarily, but here a tigress was more concerned about her cubs than about her own safety. She came and sat in the open to divert any attention from the nearby bush where the cubs were hidden.

21 Stalking begins
　　Tiger cubs start stalking by instinct, first for play and exploration and then in order to live. This cub, which despite its menacing appearance is only four months old, stalked me for about a hundred yards and then left off – probably because it had strayed as far as it dared from its mother.

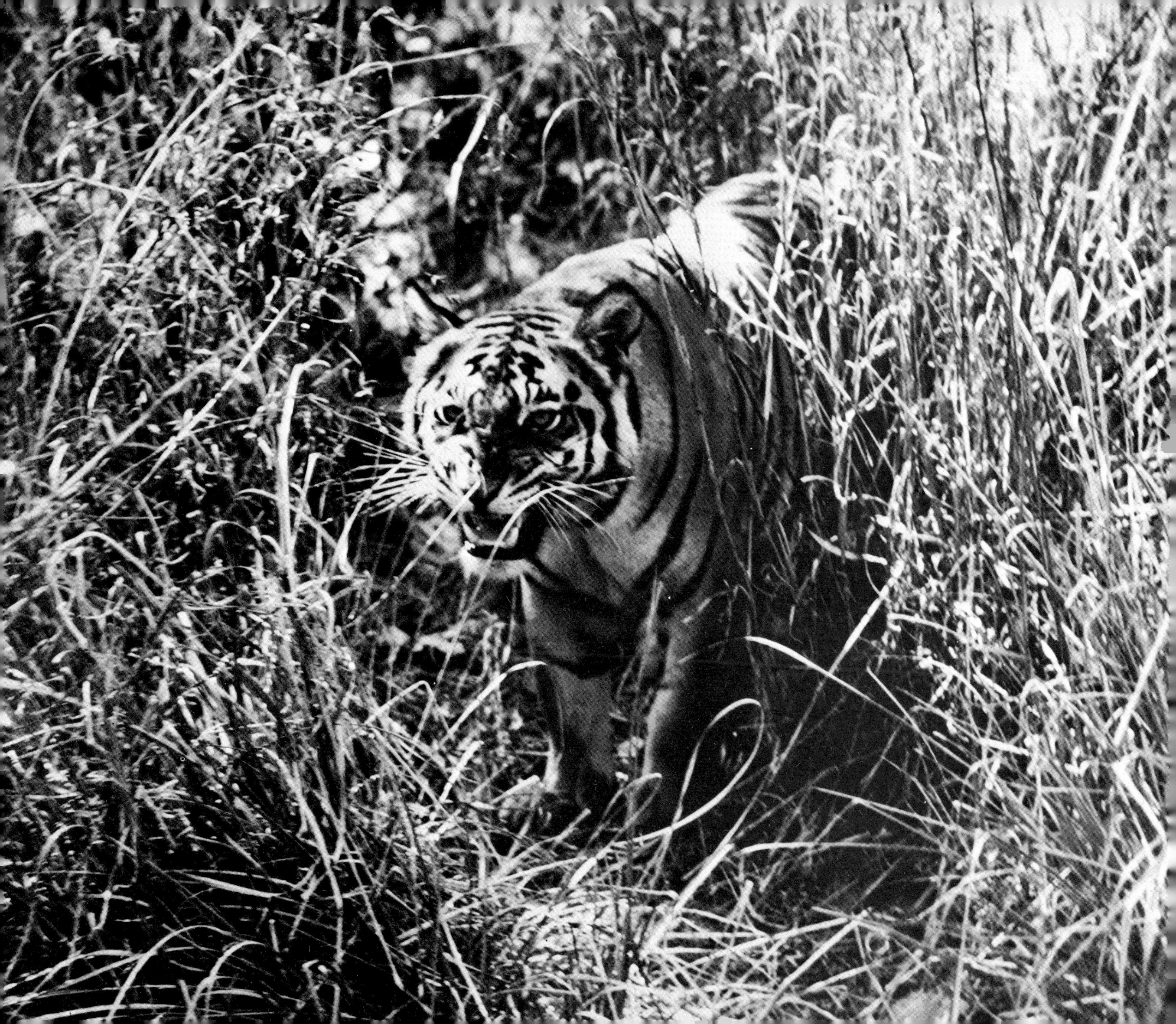

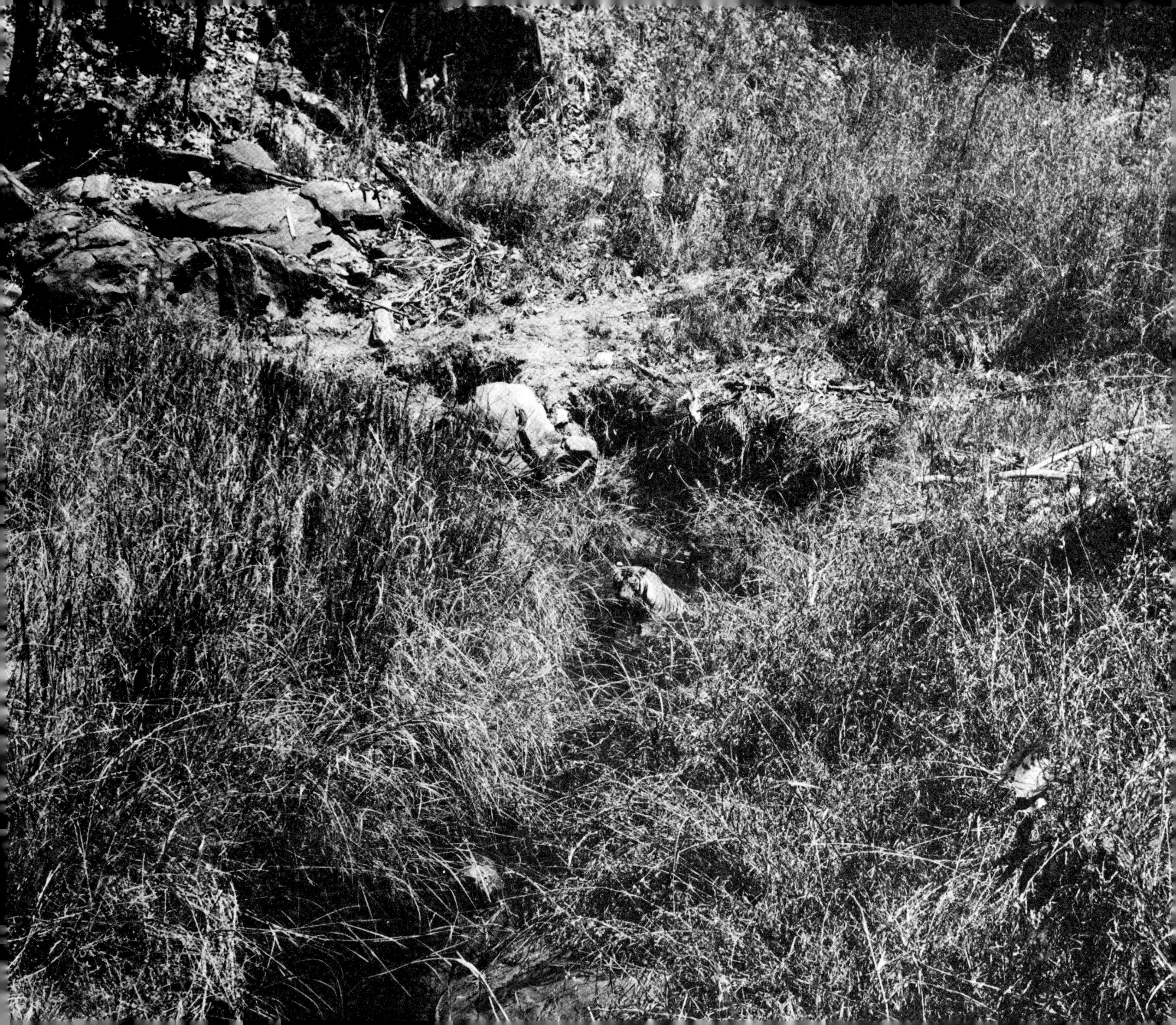

22 A perfect environment
This tiger is basking in a stream bed on a sunny winter's day. The surroundings are ideal.

23 A meal abandoned
Tigers are usually active only at night, but this tigress, besieged by hungry cubs, left them and came to her kill during the day. After making numerous attempts to drag the carcass to cover, she eventually gave up and called her cubs to feed in the open. I caught her on her way back to her cubs.

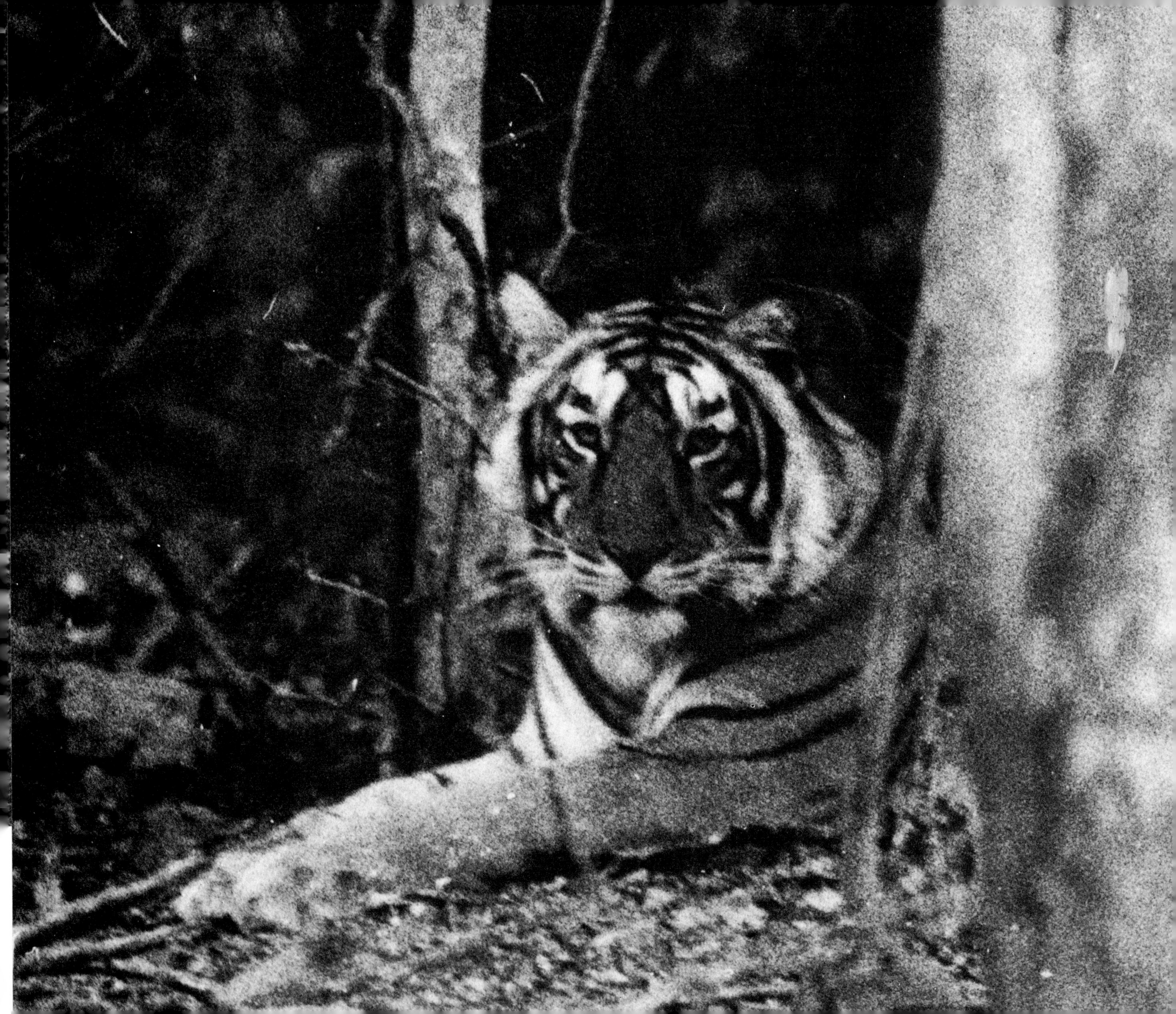

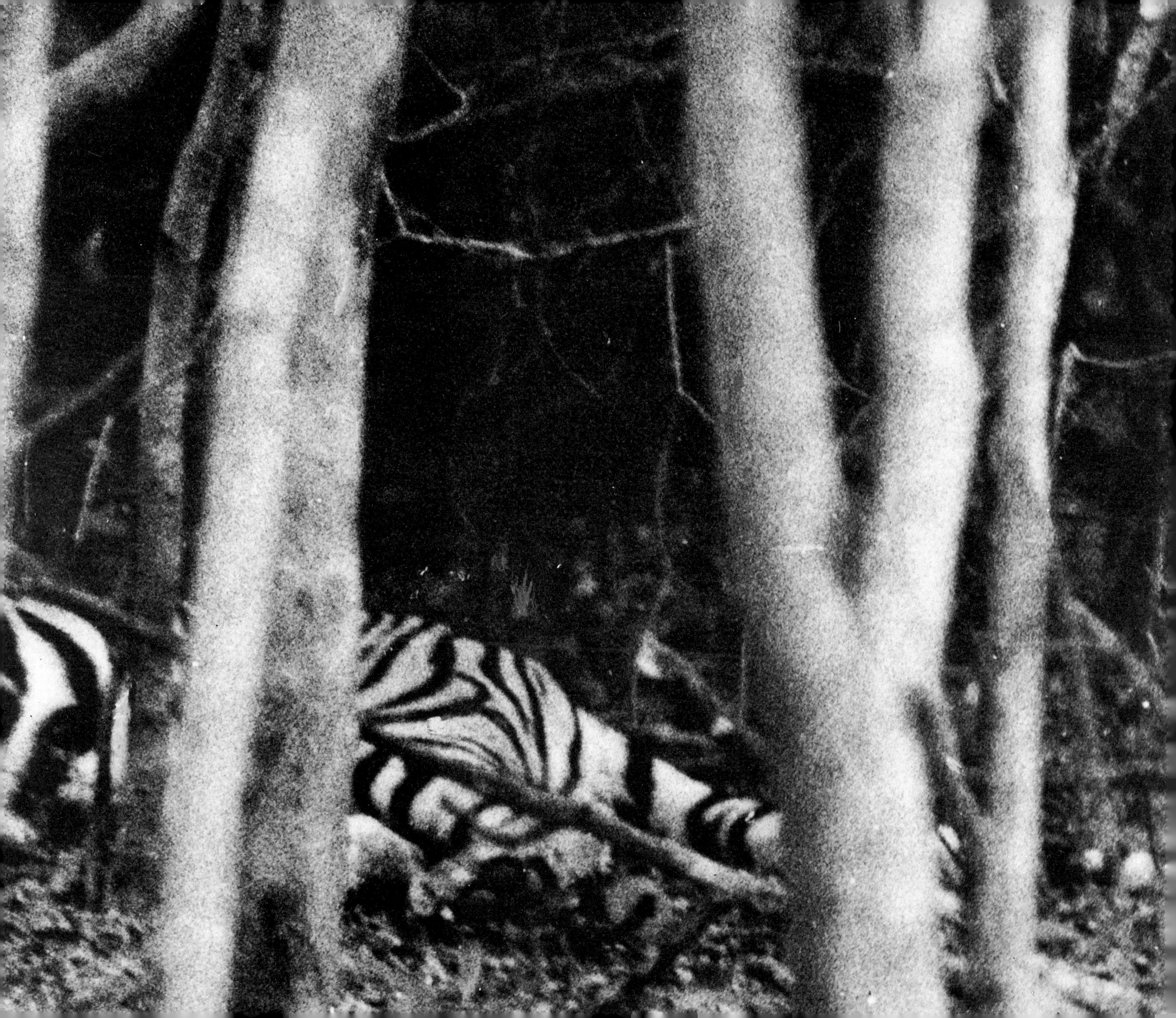

26 At rest in the forest *Previous page*
A tiger sits in the dry deciduous forests of Ranthambhor. The trees are leafless, and the tiger can easily be seen – a disadvantage when he is on the hunt, since he will quickly be spotted by his prey.

27 Tigress
The position of her tail and expression on her face indicate surprise and uncertainty.

28 Do tigers eat grass?
Yes! As this picture shows.

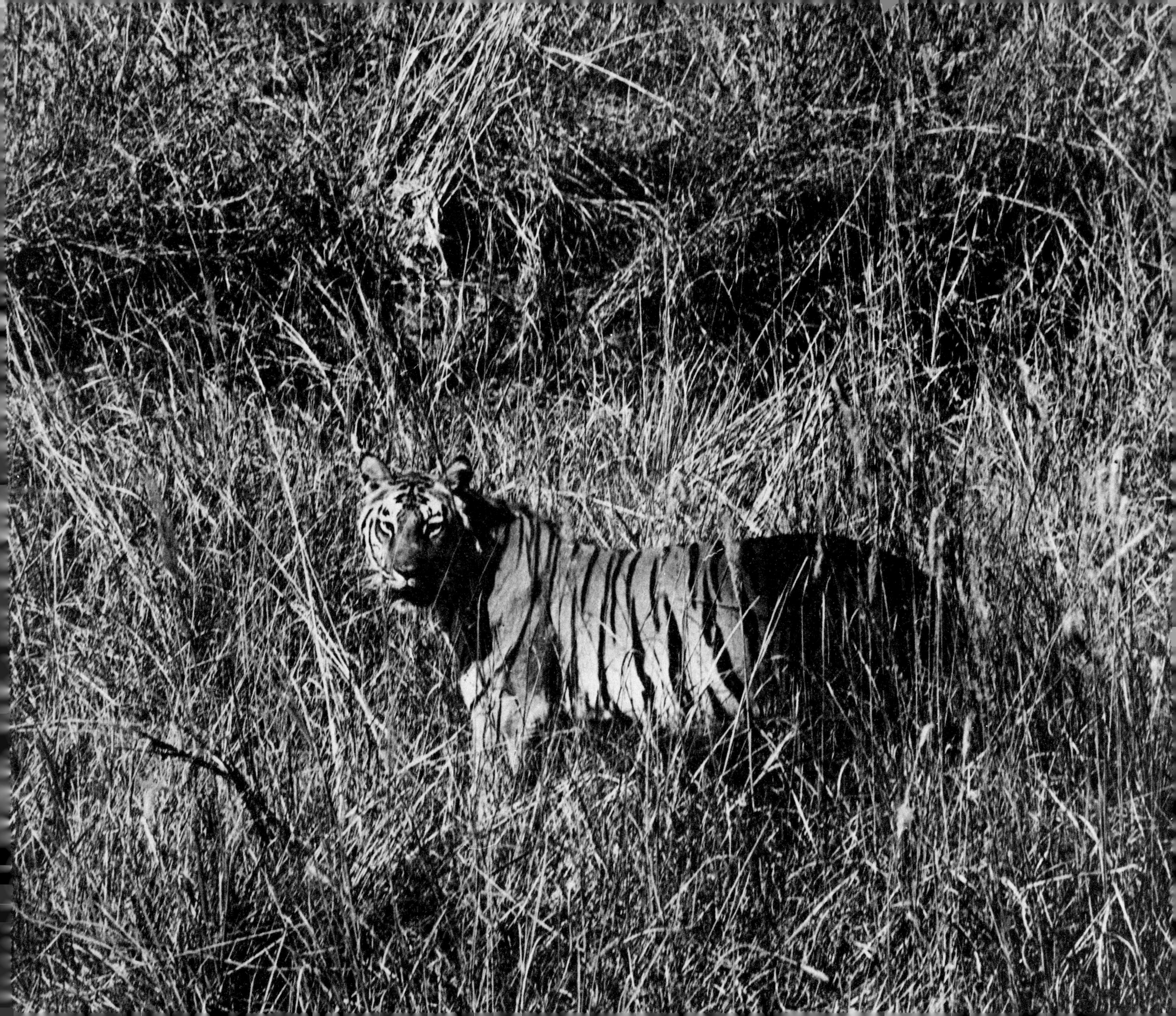

29 Tiger in the grass
Grasslands are ideal places for tigers because they provide perfect camouflage.

30 Top view
Tigerland is not only the preserve of tigers. Here a leopard has climbed a tree, which he will do with all the ease of a cat. He carries his kill to feed on it at high table beyond the reach of a hyaena or even a tiger, who are both apt to poach his food. He also takes a top view to spy out the movements of his prey. His speed in climbing trees makes him the principal enemy of langurs and peafowl.

33 Coffee break
A troupe of langurs avoid the hot sun in the patchy shade of thorny shrubs. They are of all age groups, ranging from a few days old to the most elderly, including the dominant troupe leader and a harem of females.

34 A family scene
Female langurs are very maternal. Young babies will cling to their mother's breast with such tenacity that the mother can jump over obstacles without difficulty. The mother's feelings are very strong, and if one of her children dies she will carry it in her arms for days.

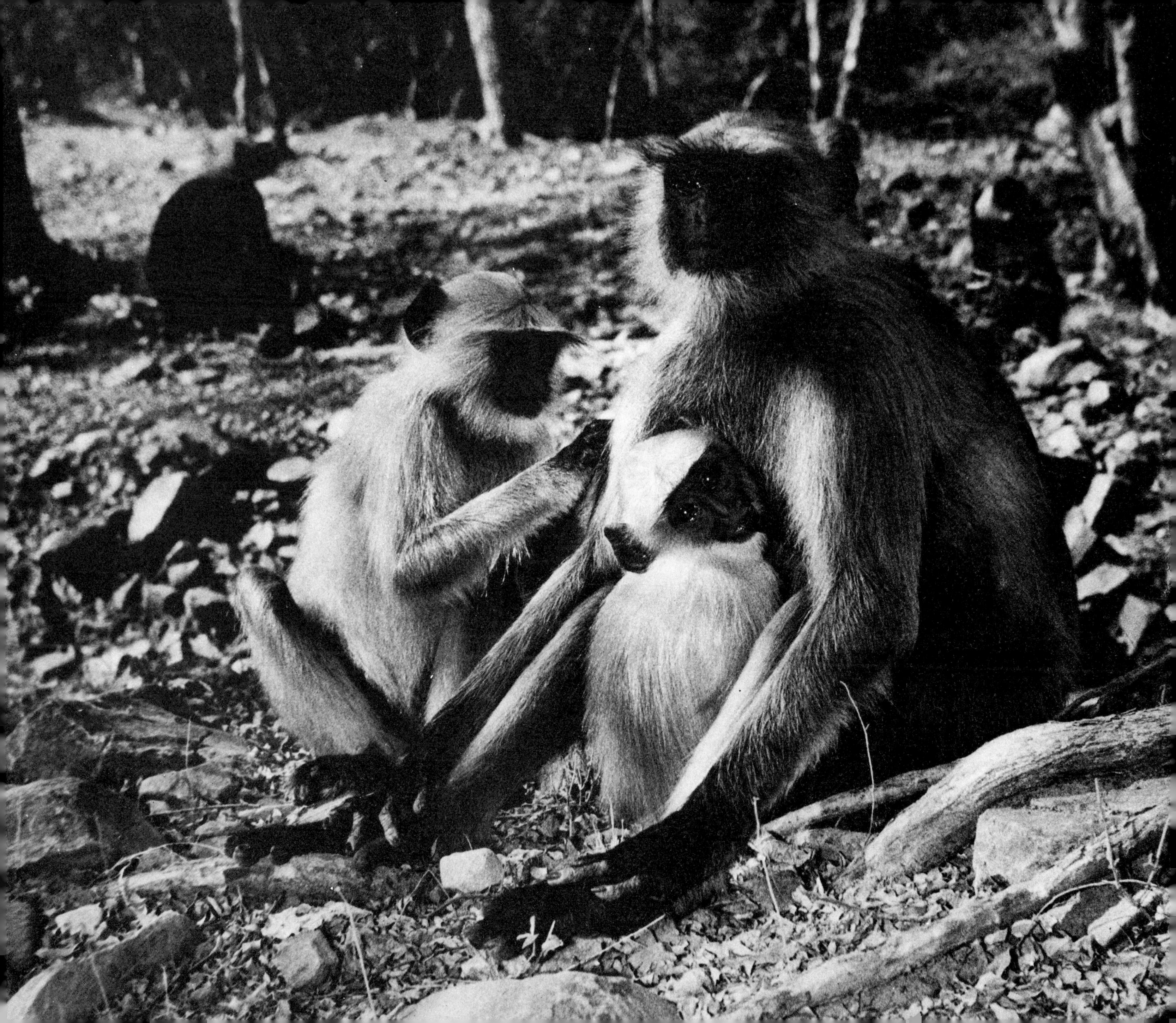

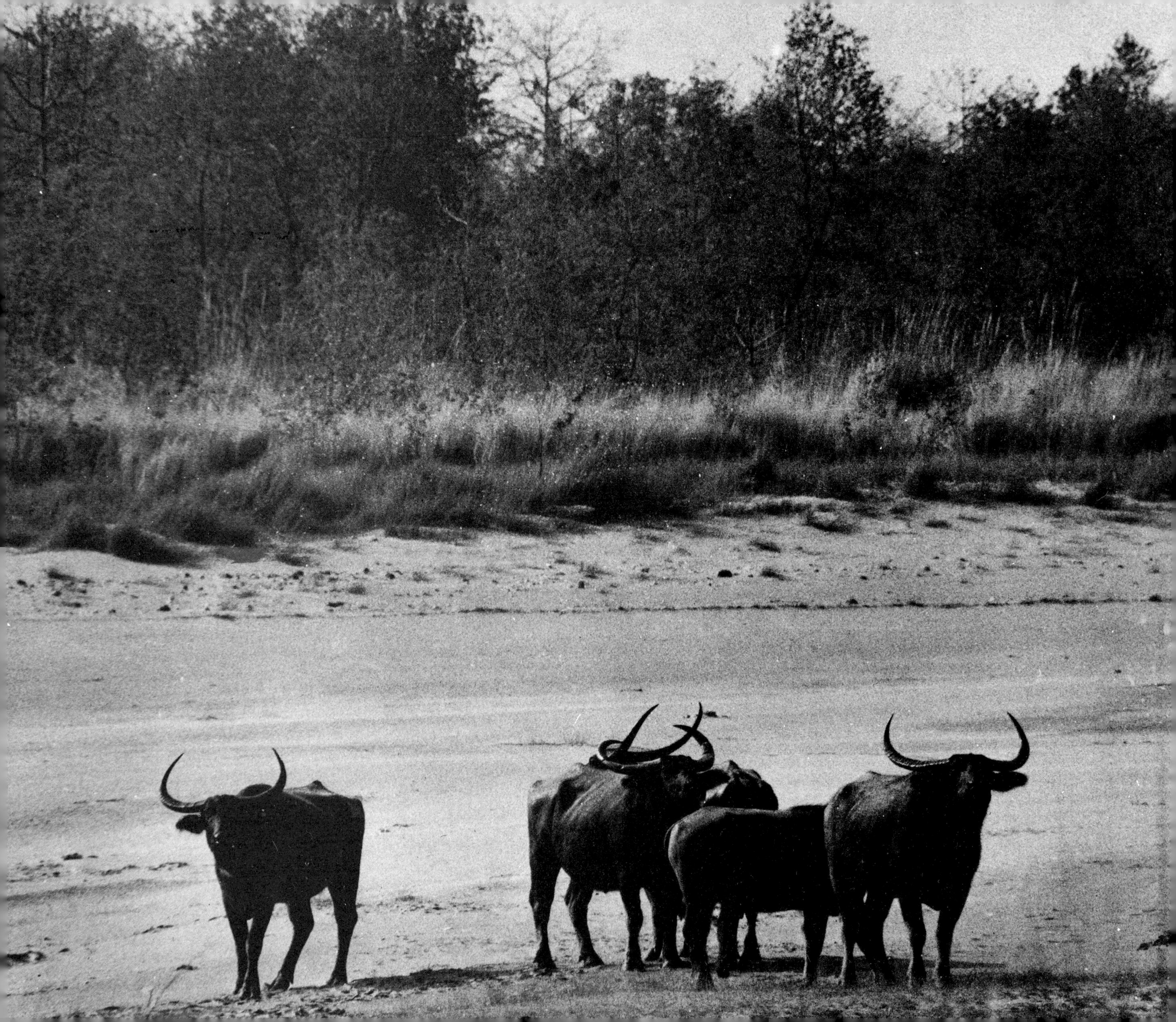

35 Wild buffalo
Sometimes individuals separate from the herd or group, but their determined stance can send even tigers bolting. When attacked they form a ring, and keep the predator at bay. Buffaloes (*bubalus bubalis*) are now confined to Manas and Kaziranga in Assam and Bastar in Madhya Pradesh.

36 Elephants in Manas
The circumstances were perfect for a good picture, but an elephant does not pose willingly, and I had to be ready for a quick exit. The Indian elephant (*elephas maximus*) is smaller than his African cousin. The Indian elephant differs from the African, having a smaller body, ears and tusks. All cow elephants are tuskless.

37 Tusker at large
It is dangerous to take liberties with lonely tuskers, as they are notorious for their uncertain moods and vicious behaviour. If the photographer's jeep fails to start or the gears get jammed, the consequences may be disastrous. The Himalayan ranges are the typical features of the landscape of the foothills in the Park, where elephants can still roam freely.

38 Love Jumbo-style
An unusual shot of courting elephants, taken against the background of Corbett National Park.

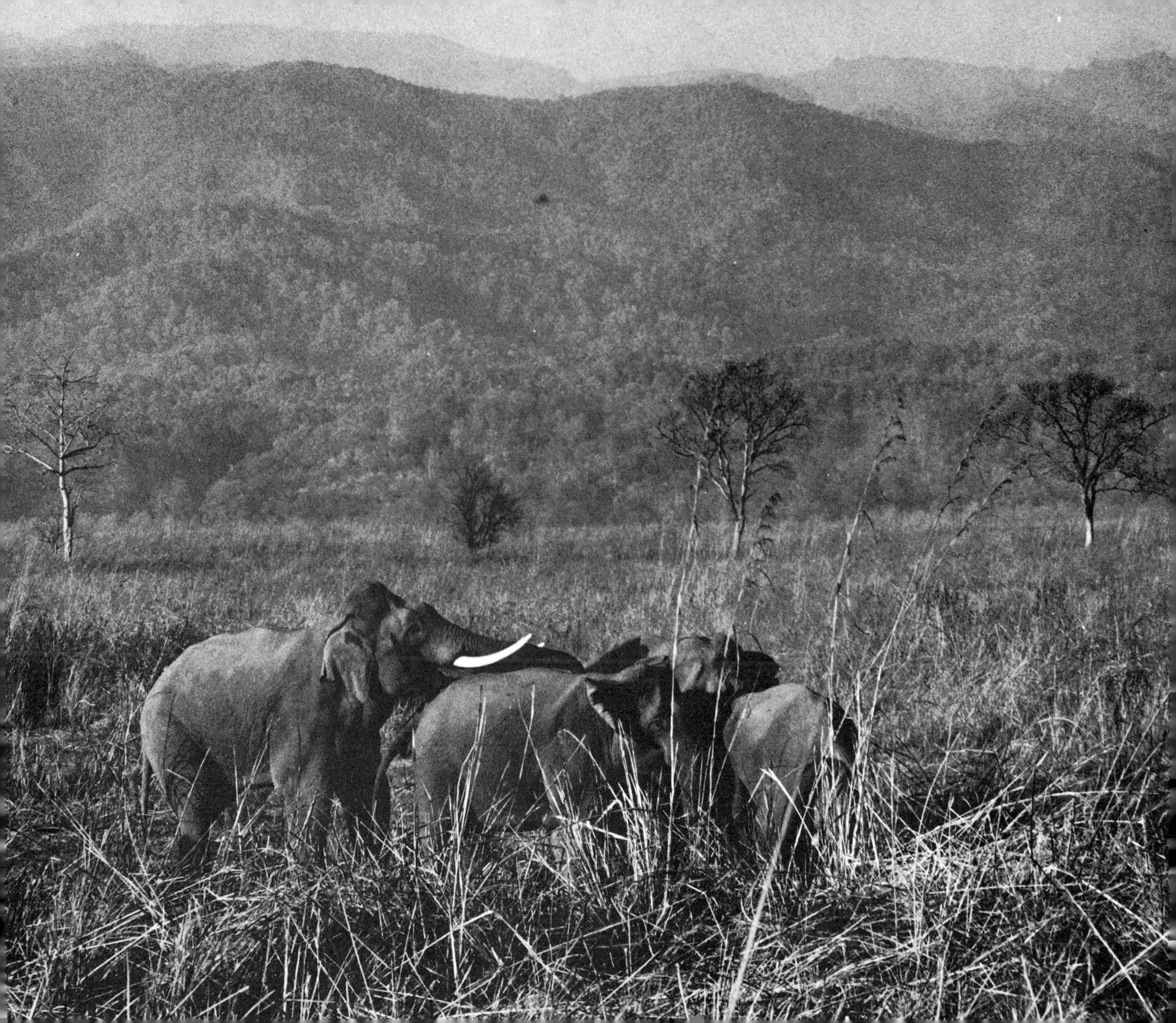

39 I told you so!
Everyone photographs a peacock with its tail feathers spread, but peahens can also be photogenic. These two were snapped with the help of the last rays of the setting sun. They came close to my hide, and were discussing their misgivings about my presence there.

40 Saras crane
This bird (*grus uncolor*), feeding in pairs, dominates the North Indian landscape. It will travel to the open fields, river beds and pools where it finds grain, frogs and snails. The cranes gather together, dance and then settle in pairs for the summer. Family responsibilities are shared by mother and father and, when one relieves the other, the scene resembles the Changing of the Guard, with trumpeting and a short dance.

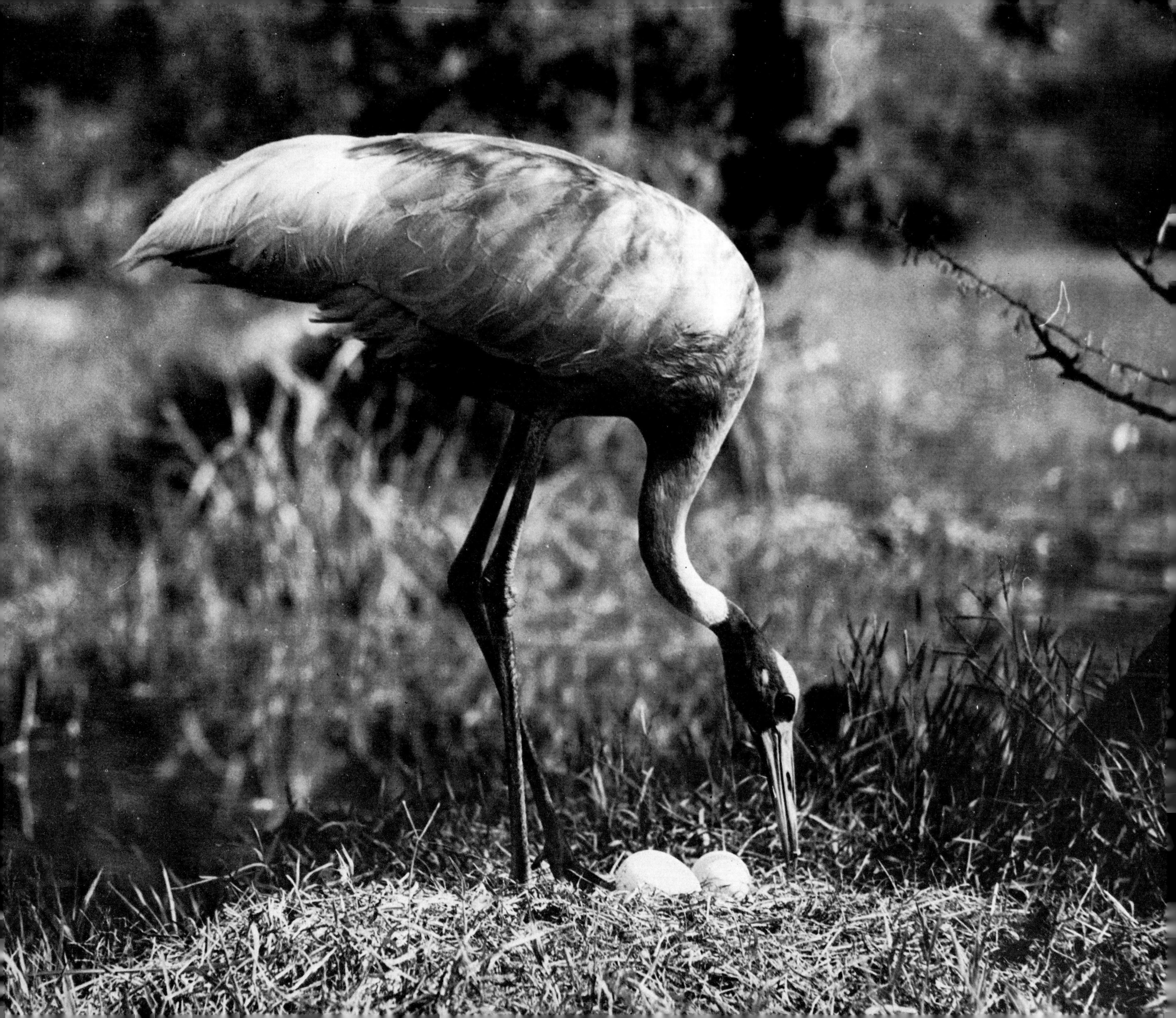

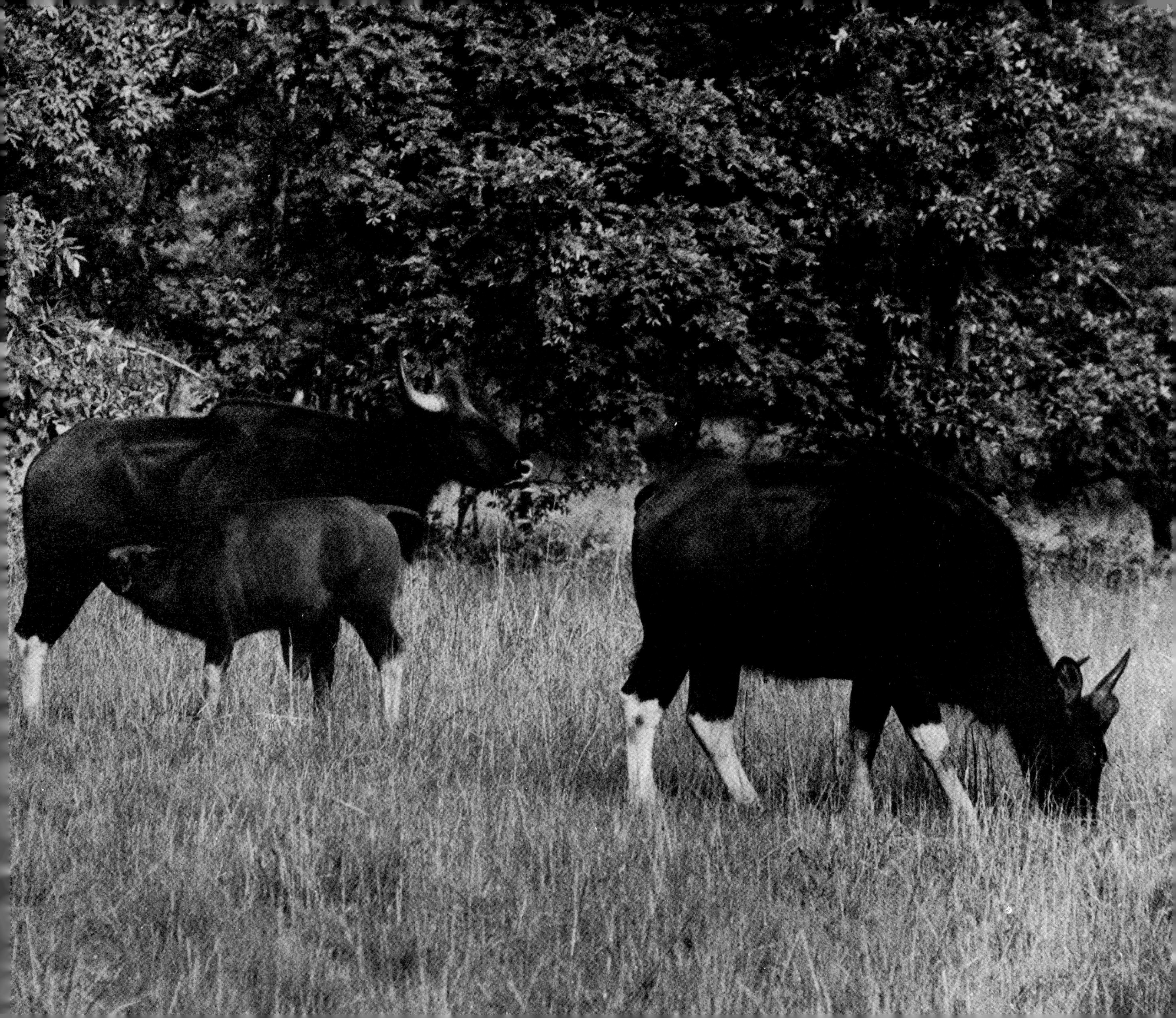

41 Gaur
  The Indian gaur (*bos gauvus*) is mistakenly called bison, just as the American bison is wrongly called buffalo. Gaur pass most of the day resting in the woods and emerge in the evenings to graze. The herding habit is their main defence, as their enemies are then unable to select and isolate an individual beast.
  The gaur is an animal of the woods. It comes out in meadows only in the late evening, and is therefore difficult to photograph. A picture of a mother and a calf in the open is rare, and requires hours of stalking and preparedness.

42 Sambar stag
  This stag was courting a doe but obligingly turned round for a full face photo.

45 Mock battles
Survival of the fittest is nature's law. But in swamp deer stag parties the combats are often only for fun. Even a third member of the group may be willing to join in the game.

46 A proud stag
A courting chital stag following a doe in heat was a good subject for a photograph. He stopped and obliged, but she took no notice. Courting chital are a common sight during the spring.

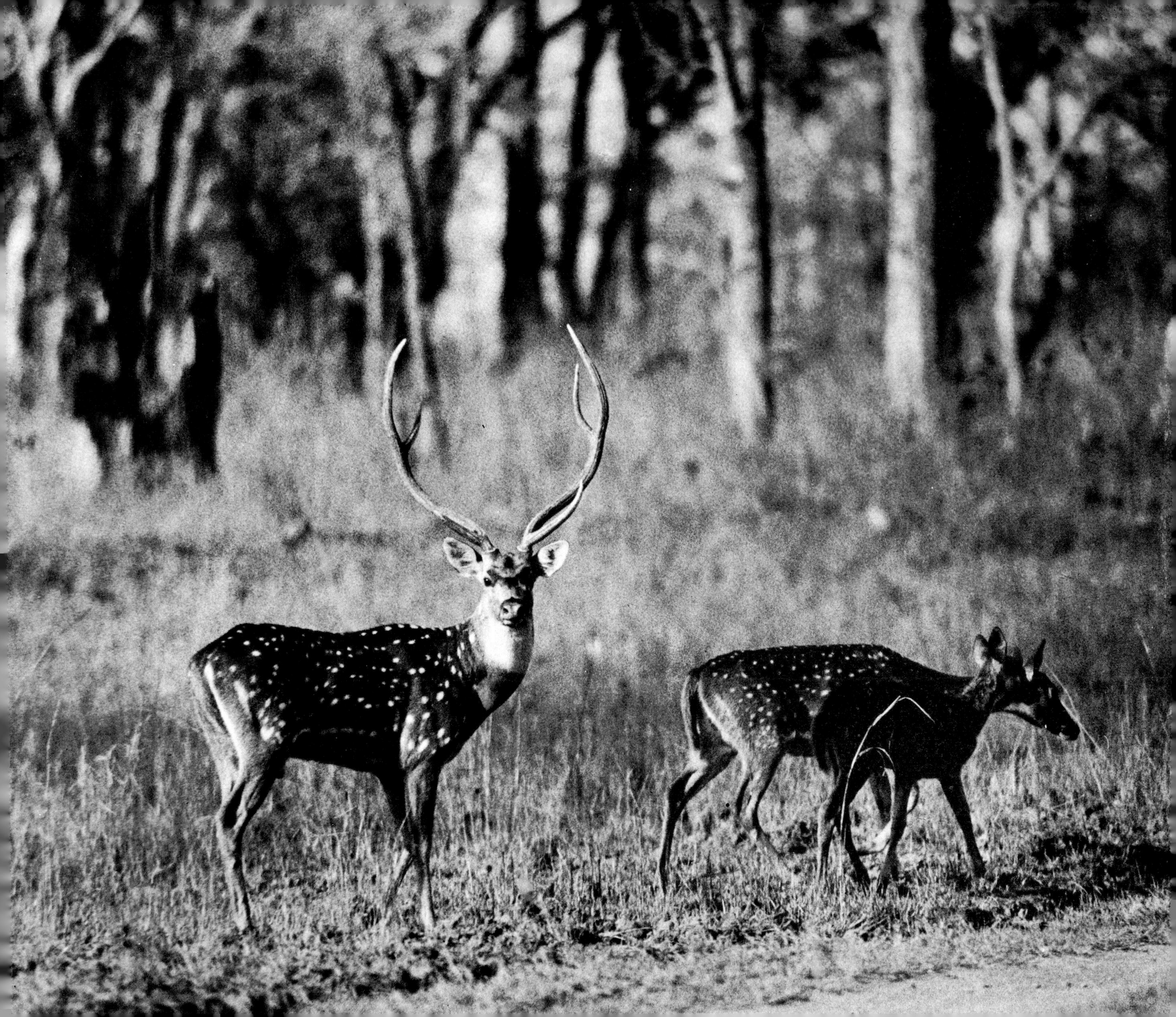

47 Co-existence
Chital (*axis axis*) and the common myna live in perfect harmony. The birds feed on parasites on the animal's body, and so relieve it of itching pains.

48 Silver lining
The antlers in velvet against the morning light have a halo, which enhances the beauty of this graceful chital stag.

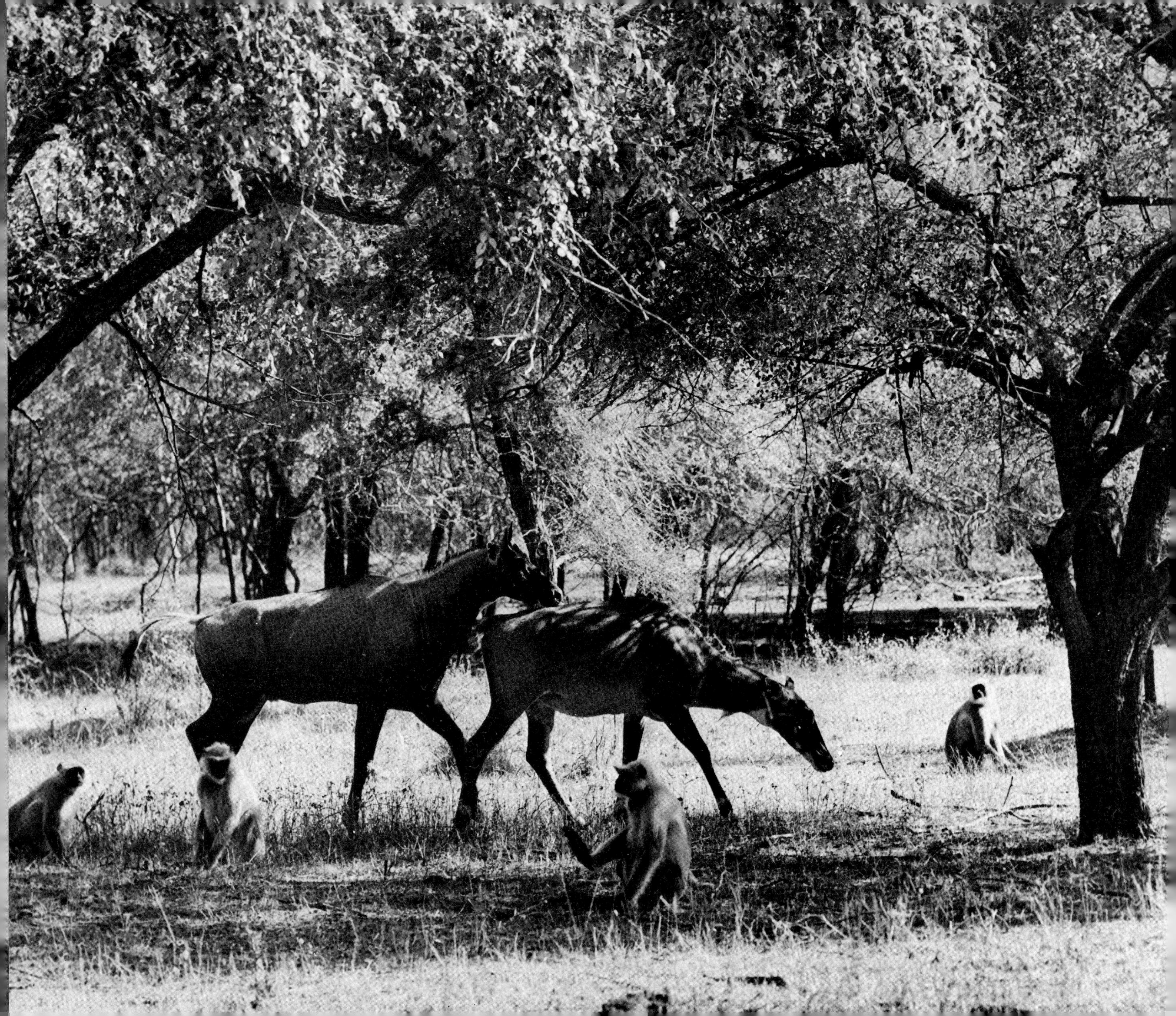

51 Love chase
As winter approaches courtship begins among the Nilgai herds. Here a strongly built bull courts a cow in heat, at the same time keeping a wary eye out for any rivals.

52 Different perspectives
Langurs feed in the high branches of trees. Inevitably broken branches, leaves and fruit drop to the ground for others to feed upon. Sometimes their weight lowers branches to within the reach of blue bulls, so the feeding habits of one species helps the other.

53 Bull party
After mating is over the blue bulls form bull parties and the females go off on their own. These two bulls are friends during the non-mating period. If they fight it is only for exercise.

54 Prince Charming
The spots on the belly and legs show that he is still too young to be alone. Soon I discovered that his mother was not far away and he was 'understudying' her. Mark the rolling body-line from the shoulder hump to the haunches and tail. The tapering tassel of the tail is the characteristic feature of the Indian lion (*panthera leo percica*), and distinguishes it from the African lion (*panthera leo leo*).

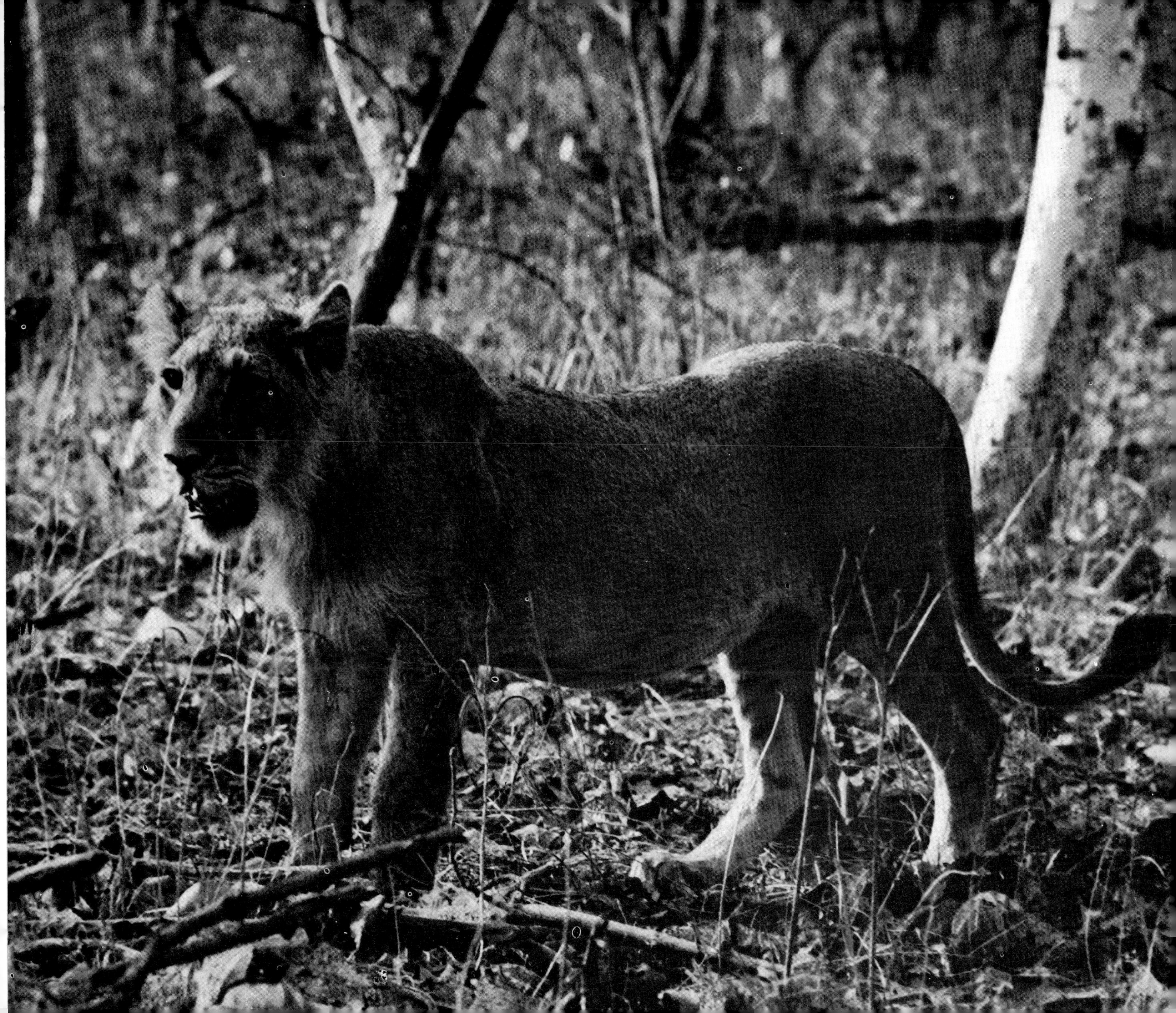

57 Jungle cat (*felis chaus*)
It feeds on small animals and birds, hunting both during the day and at night. It is a regular visitor to carcasses, and will lie in wait for the owner to take a stroll, when it will take its chance. It is distinguished by its red coat and the two rings on its tail.

58 His Majesty
The Gir lion is characterized by a scanty, unimpressive mane and tufts of hair on the elbows and the tapering tail. There are now fewer than 177 of them in the wild, and all are confined to a small forest of 500 square miles in Gir in Western India. Their dwindling number is explained by scarcity of natural prey for which they are in competition with cattle. Local people will also occasionally appropriate the kills made by the lions. I went to the Gir forests to study the habitat and to discover the reason for the total absence of tigers there. It is true that two predators who live off the same prey cannot share a habitat. The lions, who live in prides, must have driven the solitary tigers from the region. But why lions also disappeared from many other parts of India remains a mystery.

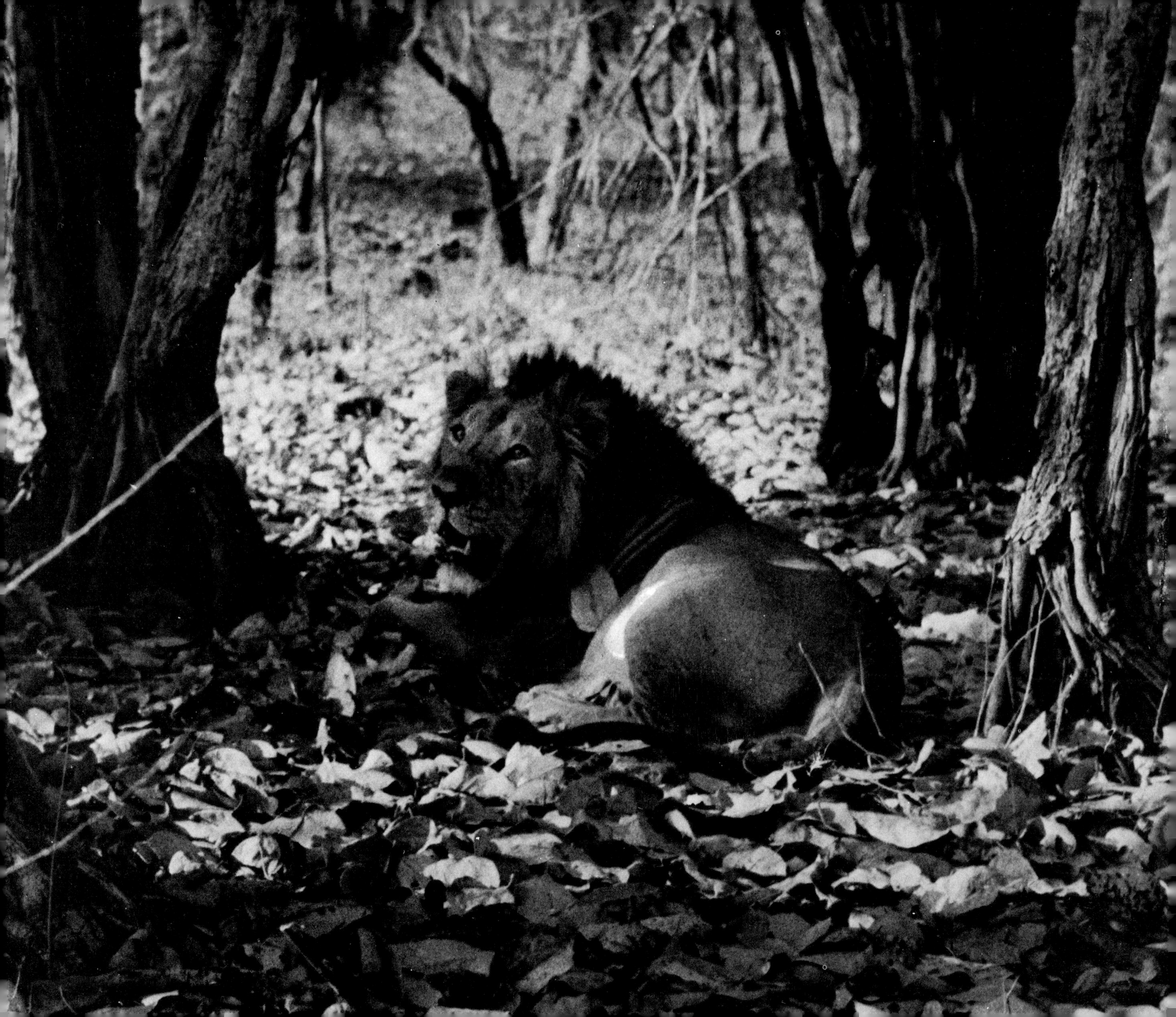

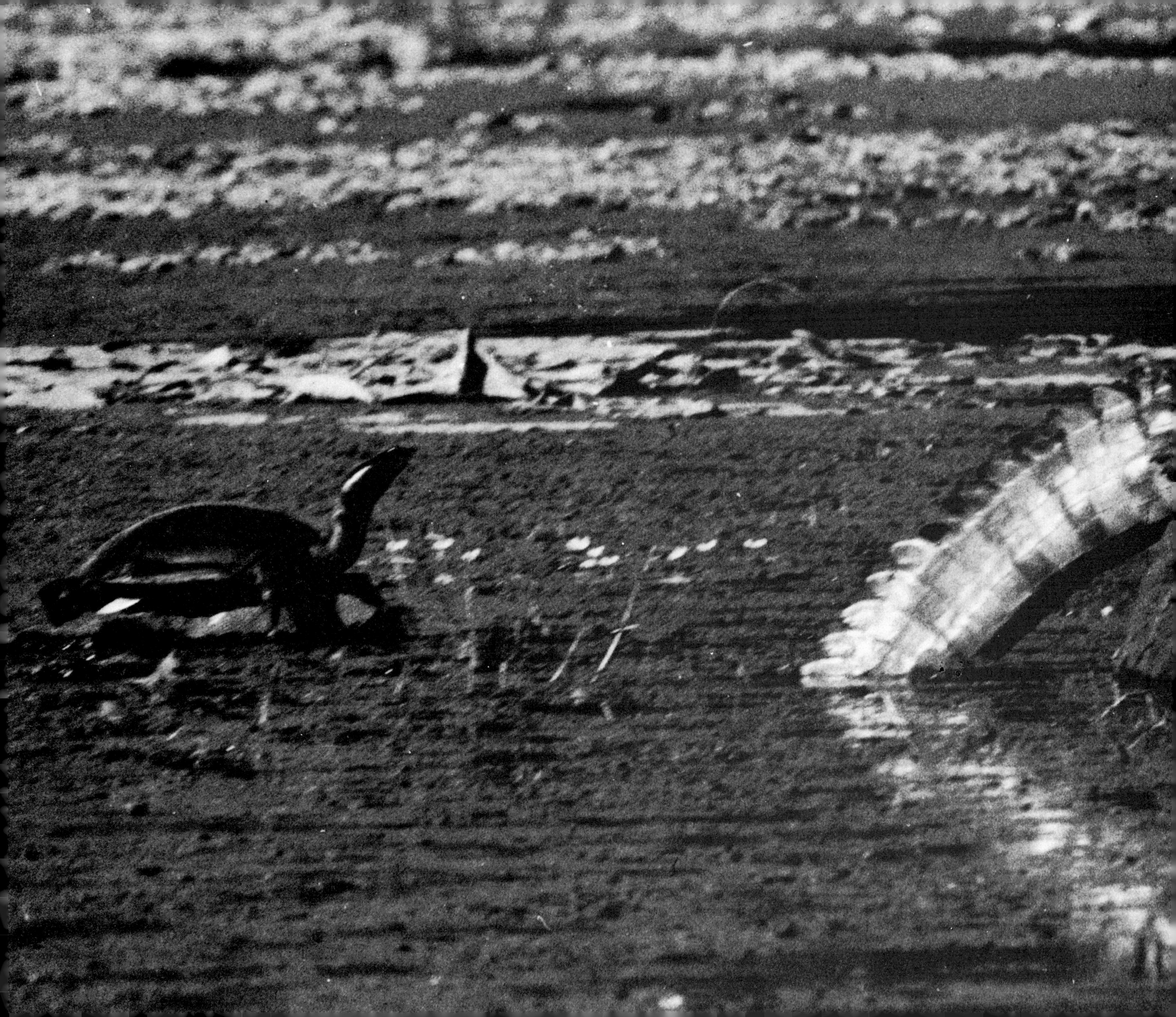

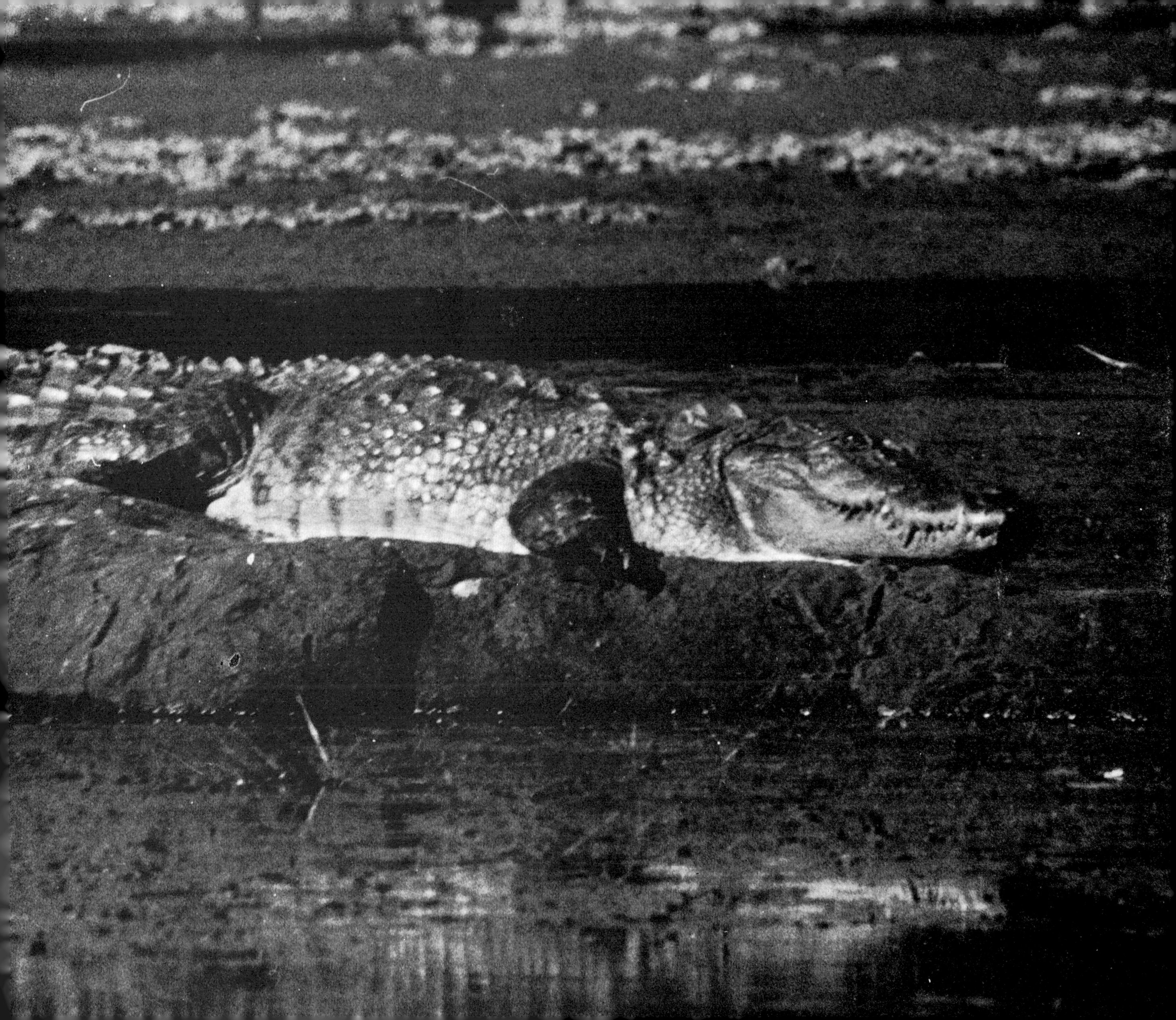

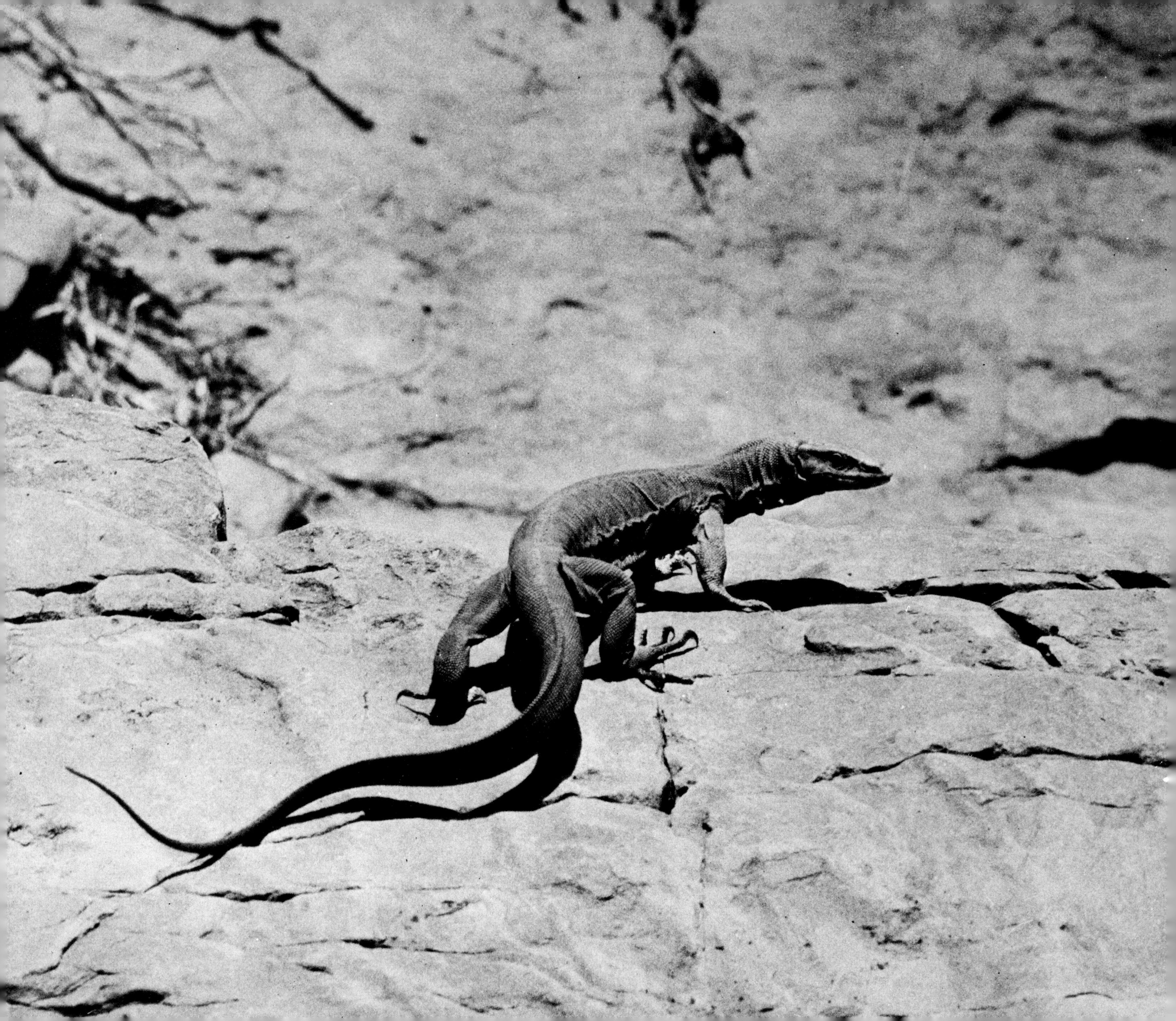

9 A friend only on land *Previous page*
A crocodile (*crocodilus palustris*) is helpless on land, but can be a nasty customer in water. He feeds mostly on fish, but lies in wait on the shore for land animals, which he drags to the water by lashing them with his tail, and then drowns them. Most of these reptiles have already been converted into handbags, suitcases or shoes. They are now rare in the lakes and rivers of India.

10 Cliff climber
The varanus (*varanus bengalensis*) inhabits rocky crevices and termite hills. This one came to feed on the leftovers of a tiger's kill, nibbled a little and left.

11 Not quite bullet-proof
The Indian rhinoceros (*rhinoceros unicornis*) differs from his African cousin in having one horn and segmented skin folds. These prehistoric-looking, armour-plated beasts are pursued mercilessly by poachers for their horns. Throughout the wild reserves of Assam and West Bengal in India and in the Terai areas of Nepal only about 700 rhinos remain. However, the last census figures (1972) show a rise in the rhino population in sanctuaries. The wet savannah of Kaziranga in Assam provides the rhino with ideal marshes for wallowing and luxuriant grassland for unlimited feeding The drango relieve them of ectoparasites and is always welcome to a ride. Egrets also perform this service.

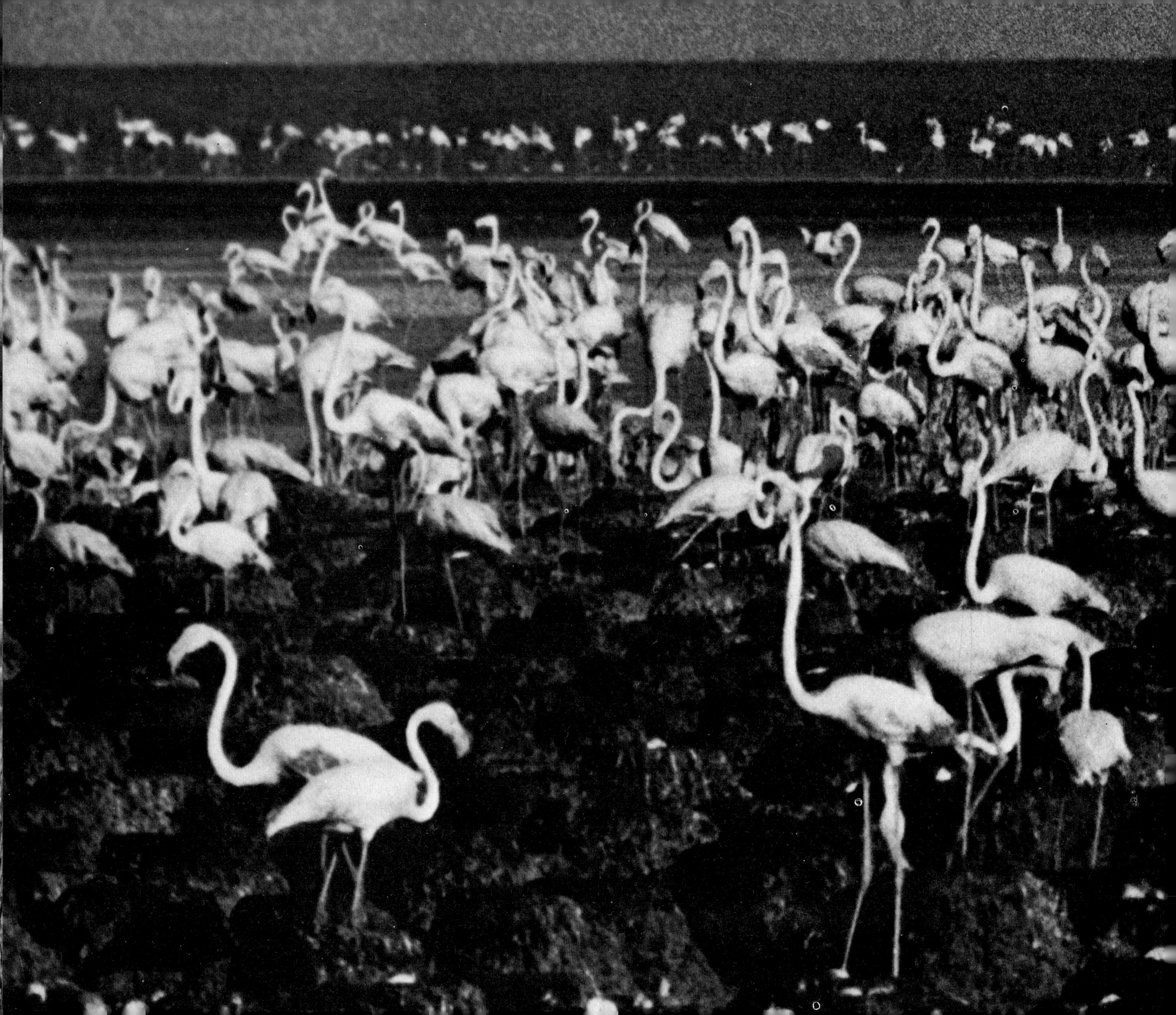

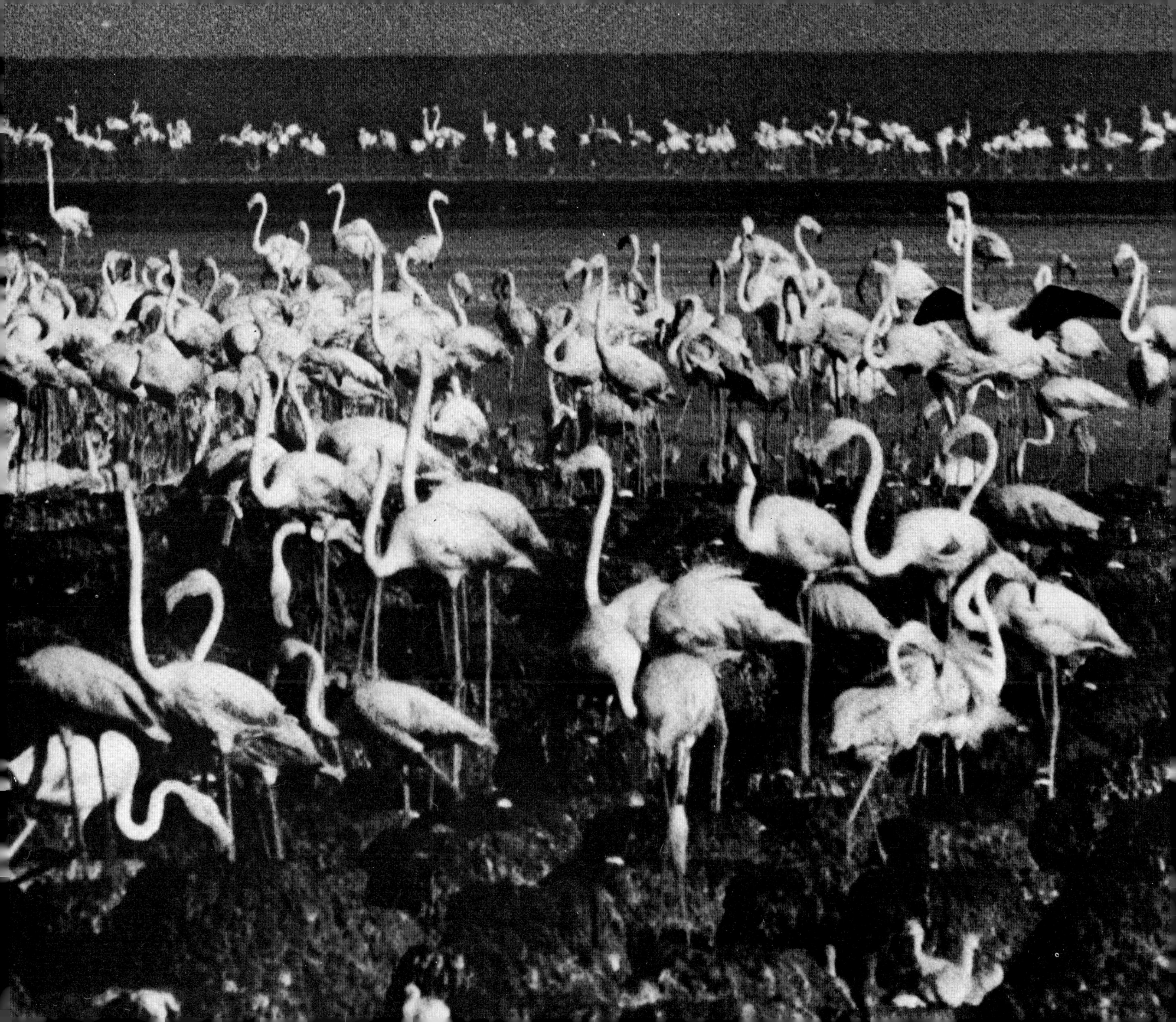

65 The stage

Waterholes at Sariska, with their background of wooded hills and palm trees, form a stage where every day the drama of nature unfolds. With sunrise the peahens and peacocks arrive. They drink, dance, fight with rivals and make love. Within an hour they have all disappeared. By breakfast time the chitals call, thirsty but watchful. They drink, stop, and drink again, as if filling up for the day. Their stay does not last more than a couple of minutes. Sometimes they are followed or preceded by the nilgai. When it is hot and the forest is quiet, the four-horned antelope arrive in pairs or family groups. A cautious blue bull arrives at tea time. At dusk sambar fill the waterhole. During the late evening the wild boars too claim their place. By dinner time come the spiny porcupines. Even tigers arrive to drink and enjoy a cool bath. If a tigress with cubs should happen to come, there will be their play to watch. Surprisingly, a waterhole is quiet at midnight except for a few visits by nilgai and sambar. Activity once again resumes at dawn till an hour after sunrise.

66 Leopards (*panthera pardus*)

I was waiting to photograph a nilgai in Bharatpur. The day was hot. There was sudden activity. A lapwing pair made restless noises. I was expecting a jackal, but instead a leopard appeared. Hardly had I clicked the shutter twice when another joined him.

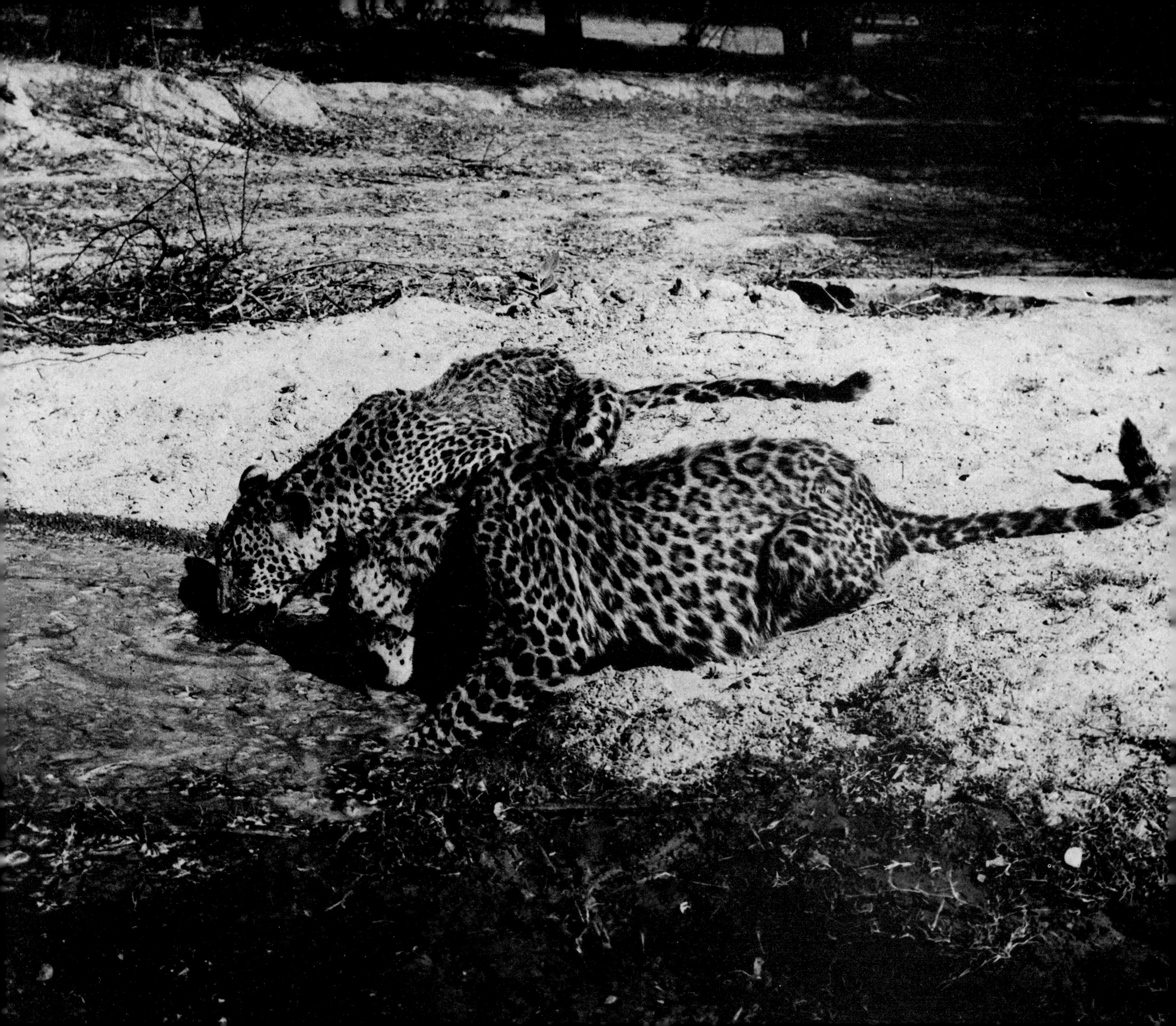

67 Wild boar (*sus scrofa*)
The boars do not mind the hot sun and arrive to drink at mid-day. The wild boar is sensitive, and has plenty of courage and determination. He fears none if he decides to fight. Sometimes there are pitched battles between a tiger and a boar – and the outcome is never certain. Even so, tigers consider pork worth the risk.

68 Reflection
The langur uses water for a mirror. In Hindu mythology one of the characters, Narad Muni, was returning from the Swayamwara (where a girl chooses her husband) and was heartbroken because he thought he was the most handsome suitor, yet returned empty-handed. On his journey home, while drinking water from a pool, he discovered he had the face of a monkey. This led to the story of Ramayana.

69 Friends *Overleaf*
If a peacock is at a waterhole it is safe for other animals to approach, and langurs will do so without fear. However, they dislike water and only touch it with their lips, never taking any form of bath. They are still the cleanest of the primates.

70 Mid-day greeting
A langur receives a peacock's good wishes. The two generally live in harmony.

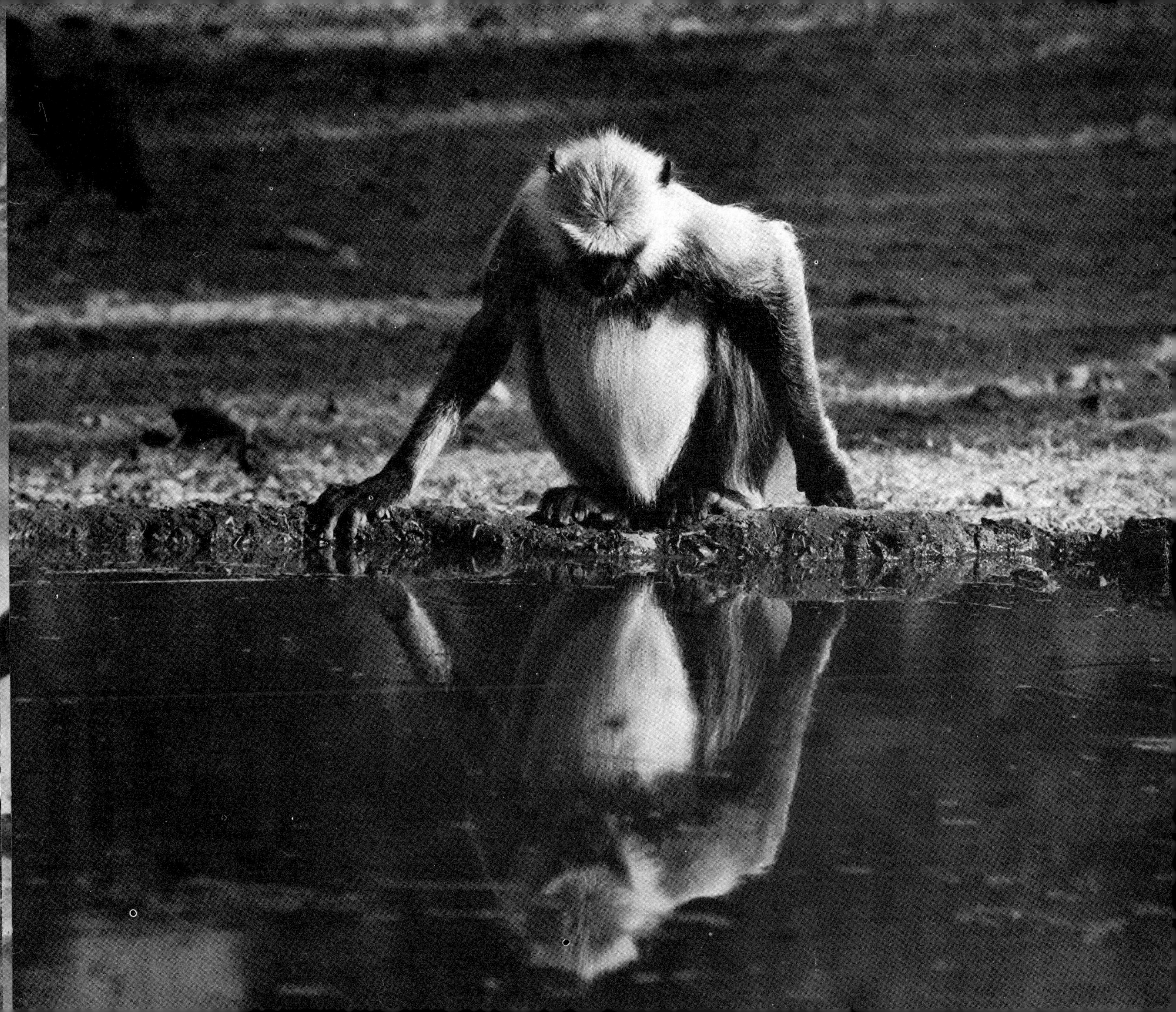

75 A water rush
This waterhole is the life-line of Kachida Valley. All animals visit it. Sambar approach timorously but, once some of them are there, the rest follow without fuss. The last member has his tail up showing his excitement at having discovered easy access to a waterhole.

76 A hitch-hiker
A sambar in summer; she does not mind entering the mud up to her knees, nor the hitch-hiking drango, who gets a free ride in return for helping to remove the doe's ticks. Sambar lose their hair and look mangy during summer, and stags lose their antlers.

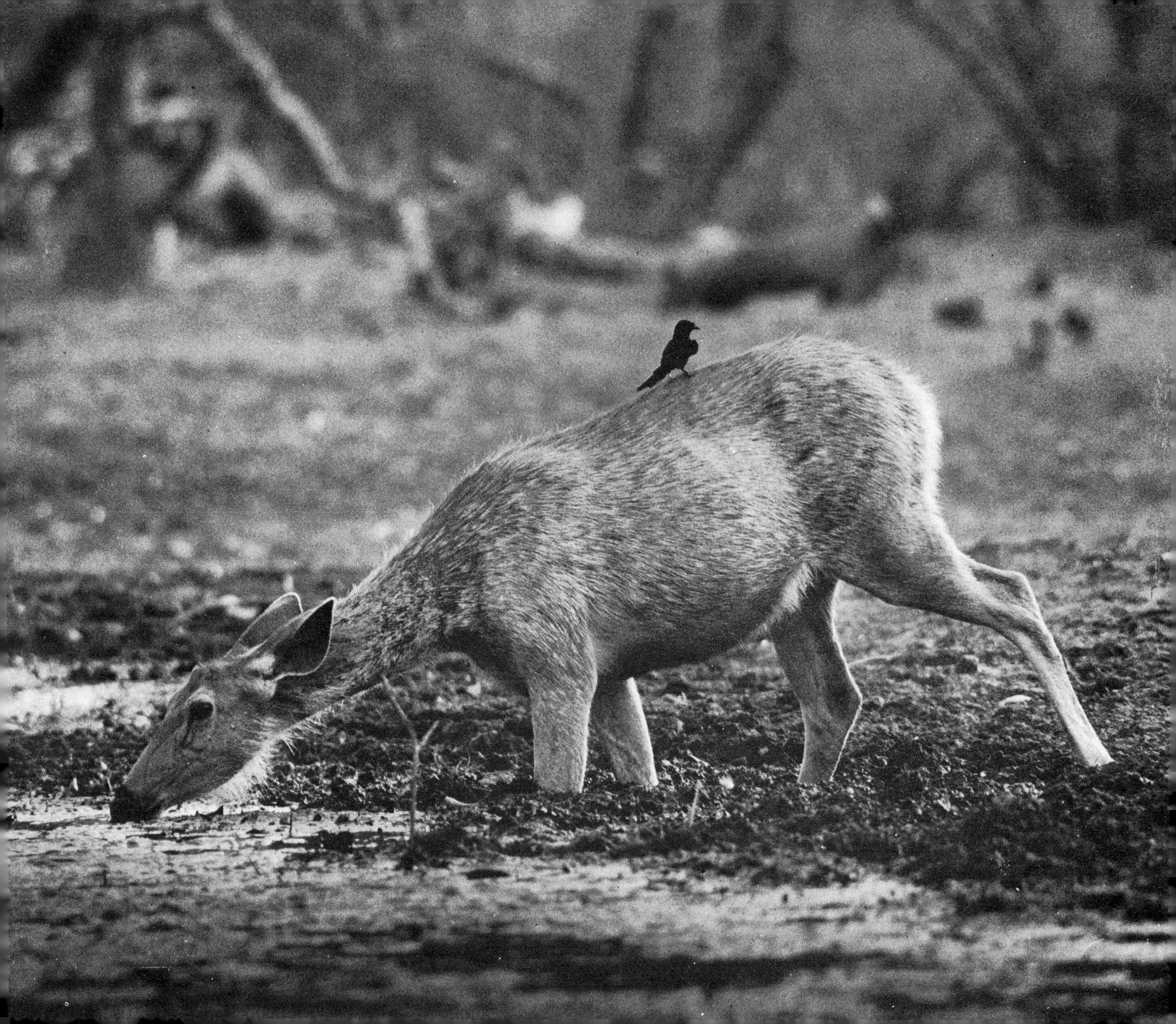

77 Time to knock off
A pair of jackals (*canis auveus*) arrive at the waterhole during the hottest part of the day, and enjoy a mud bath.

78 Happy dreams
A fine combination of whiskers and grass and a clear picture of a very handsome tiger.

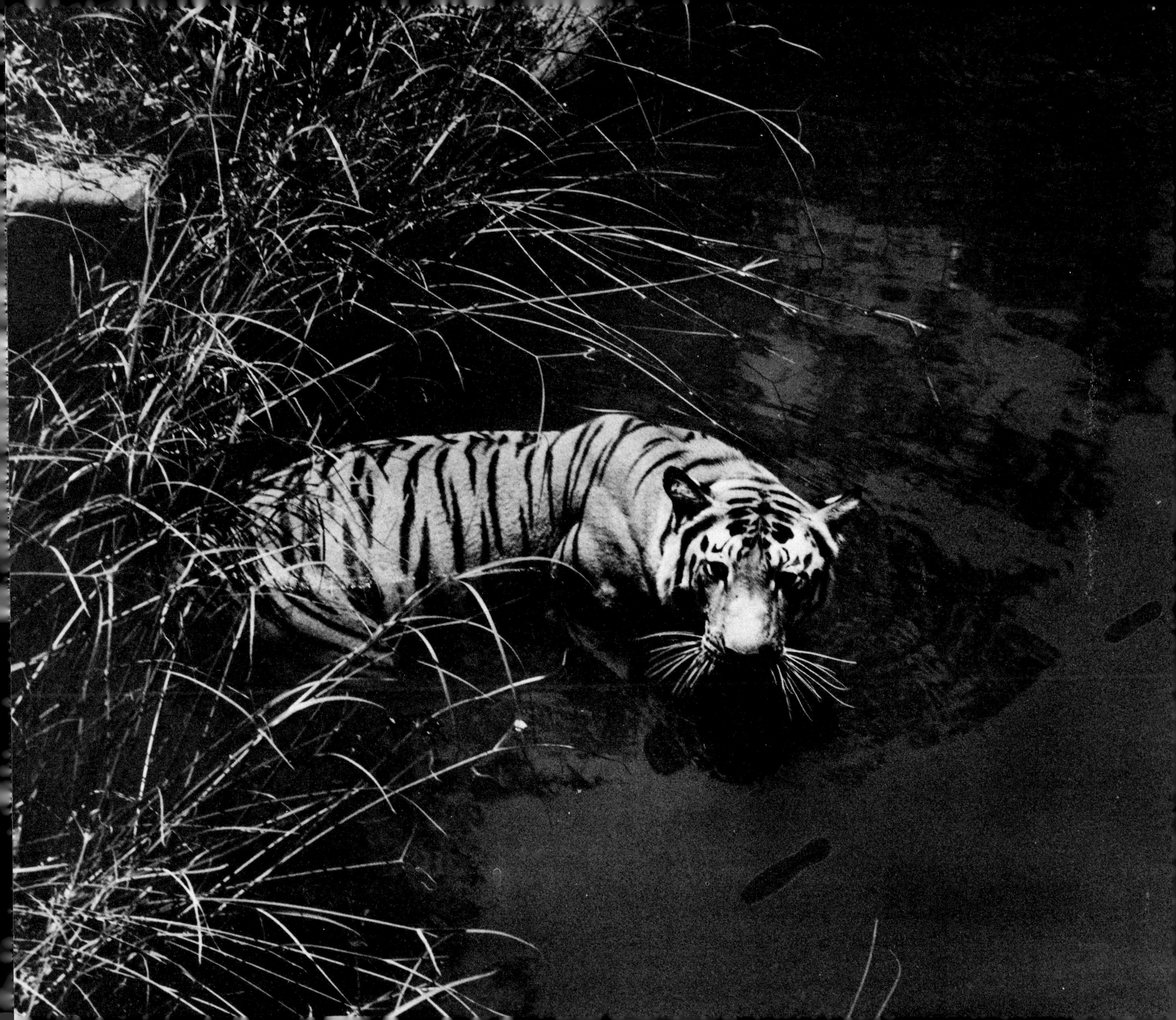

81 Musing on a rock
Occasionally he would make ripples with his tongue or tail.

82 A double image *Opposite*
This tiger was annoyed when I discovered him, and his warning whiskers forced me to withdraw.

83 Morning siesta during summer *Overleaf*
I managed a close look at this tiger while he was resting in a pool formed by the drying river bed.

84 An ideal spot
Tigers love water, both in winter and summer. Here the tigress's belly shows her in an advanced state of pregnancy.

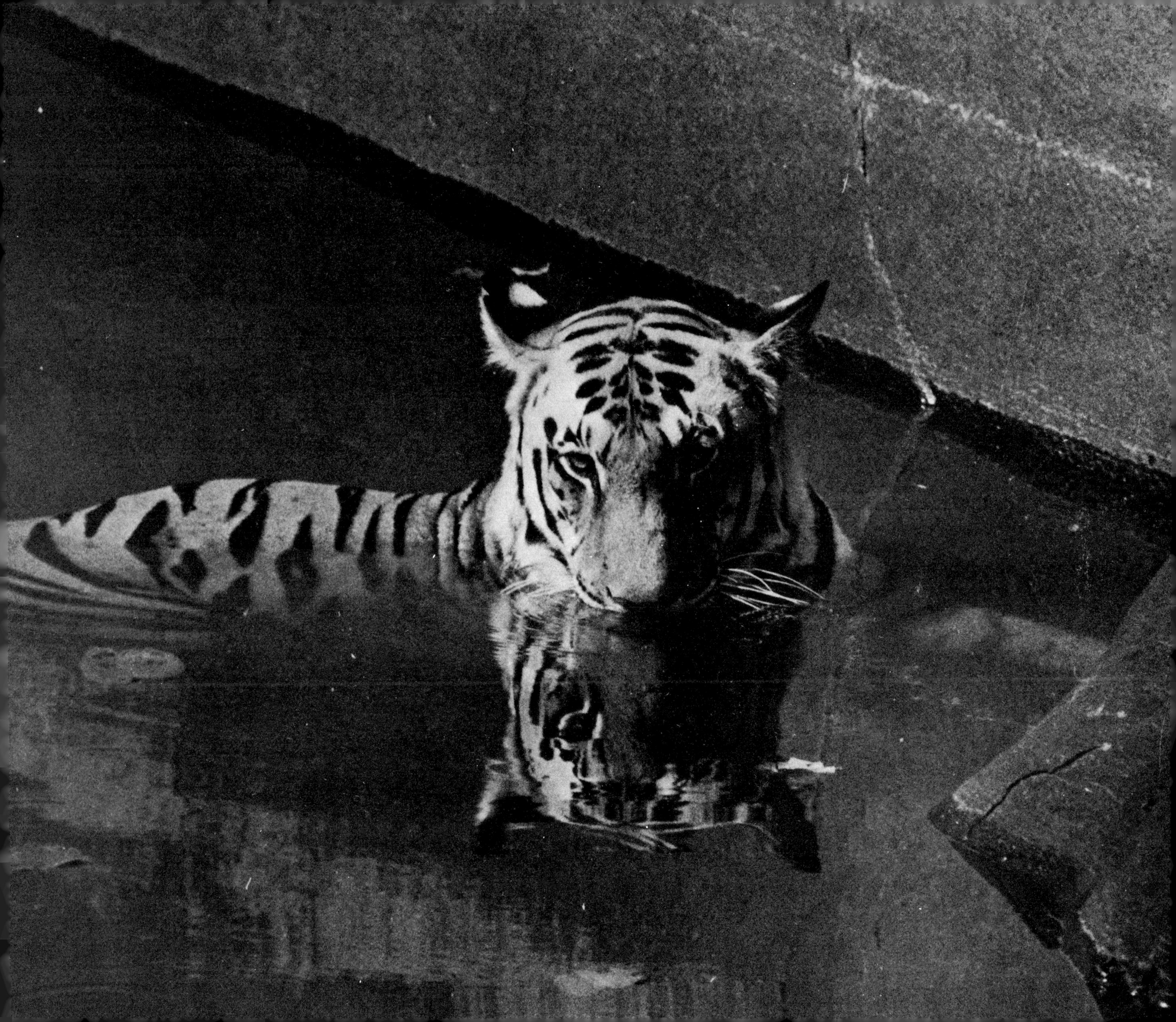

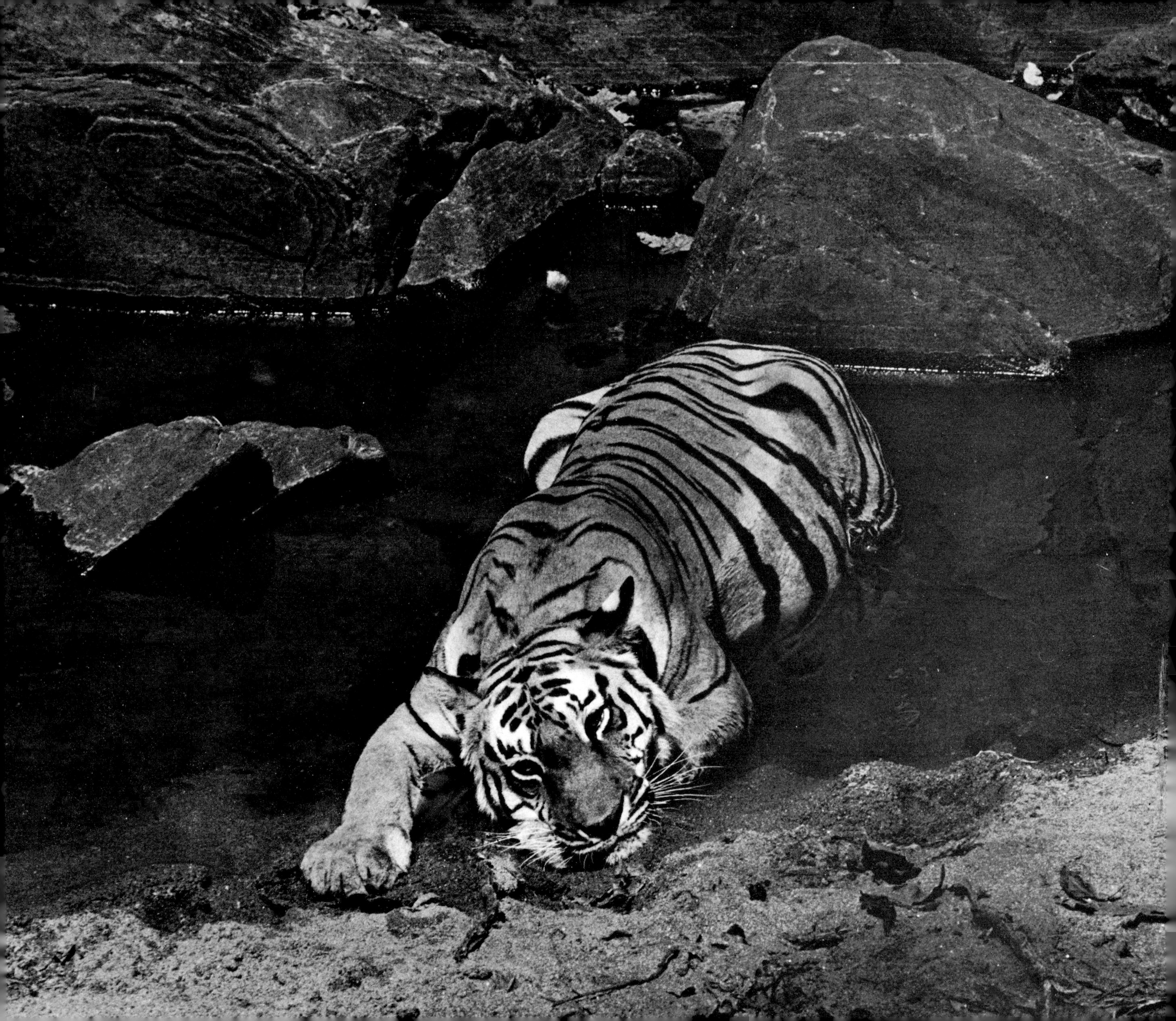

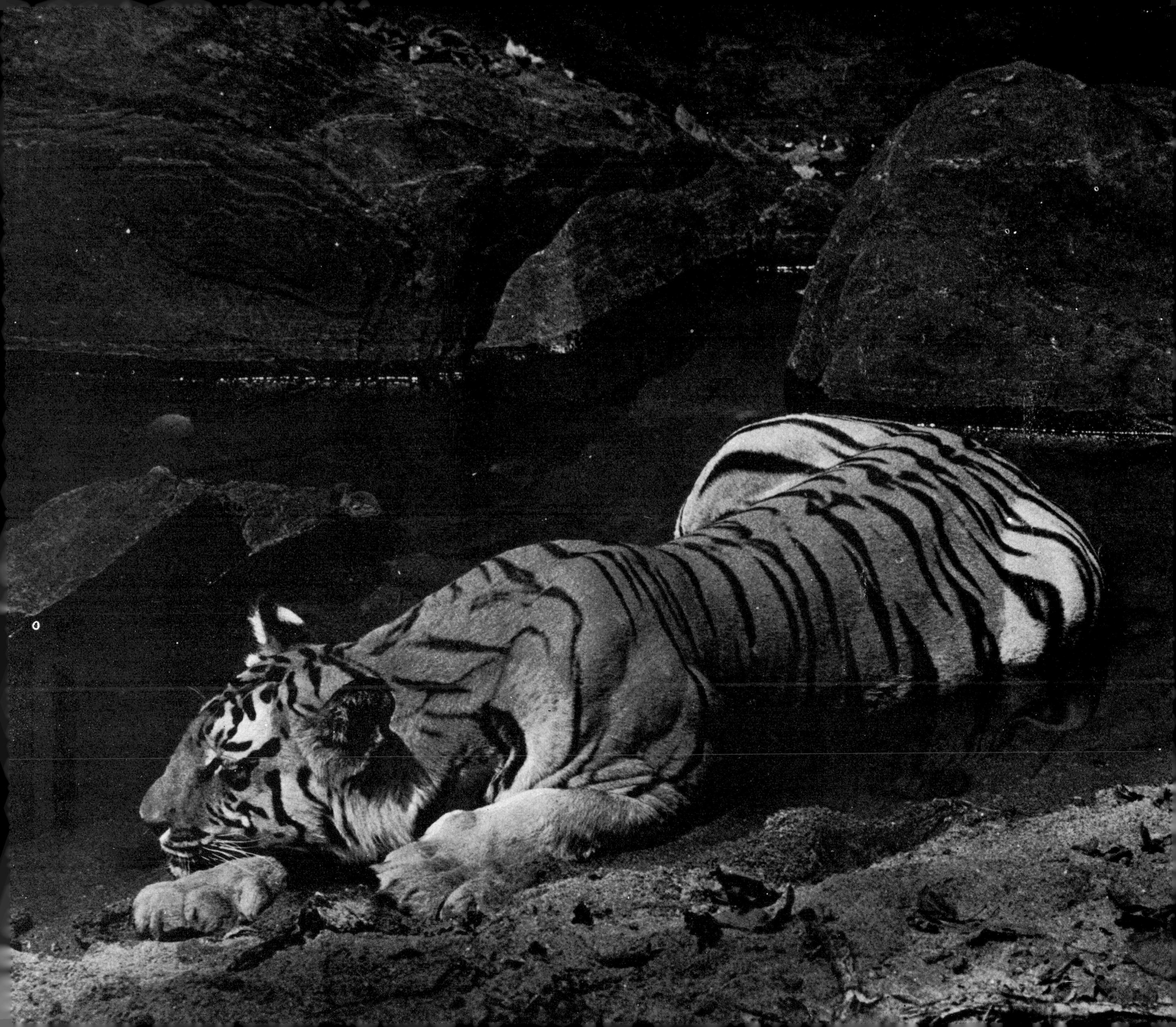

85 Peace and tranquillity
While any other cat avoids water, the tiger enjoys every drop of it. Quiet and shady pools in dry forests are a paradise on earth for tigers, and in the hot months of April and May they spend all day there.

86 A welcome bath
A sambar stag wallows in a muddy pool in the Kachida Valley.

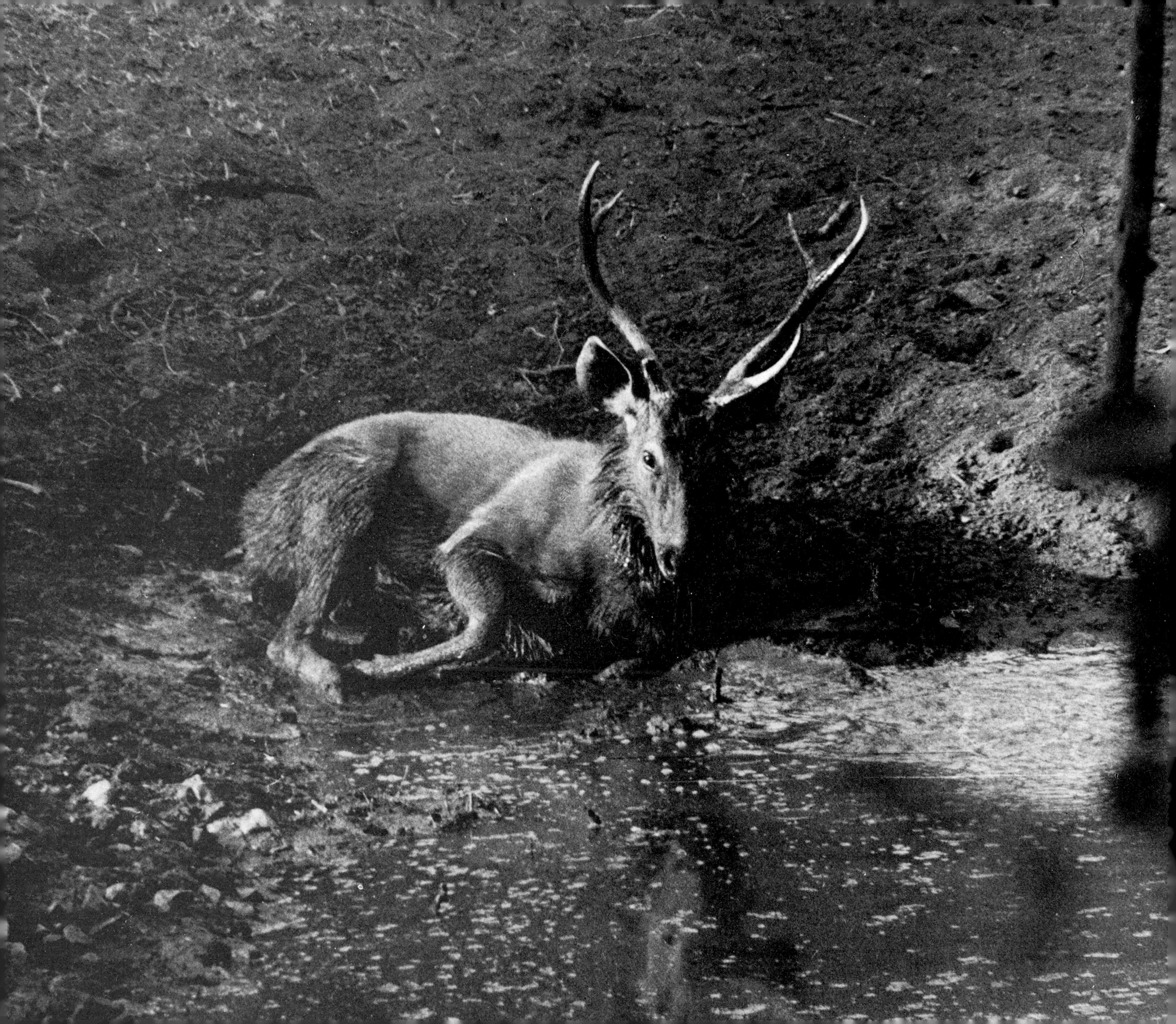

87 A sign of maturity
It is possible to tell whether a stag has reached maturity by the colour of its coat. At birth both male and female are fawn in colour, but the males will grow darker, and when in their prime will look almost blue.

88 Battle of Bharatpur
When black bucks (*antelope cervicapra*) fight pitched battles, they take no notice of the happenings around them; nothing will separate them until the battle is finished. The rising dust indicates intense activity. The black buck is the only true antelope, once found in herds swelling to over 10,000 in the plains of North India. Human population pressures have driven them within narrow confines, and man's hunger for protein has greatly depleted their numbers.

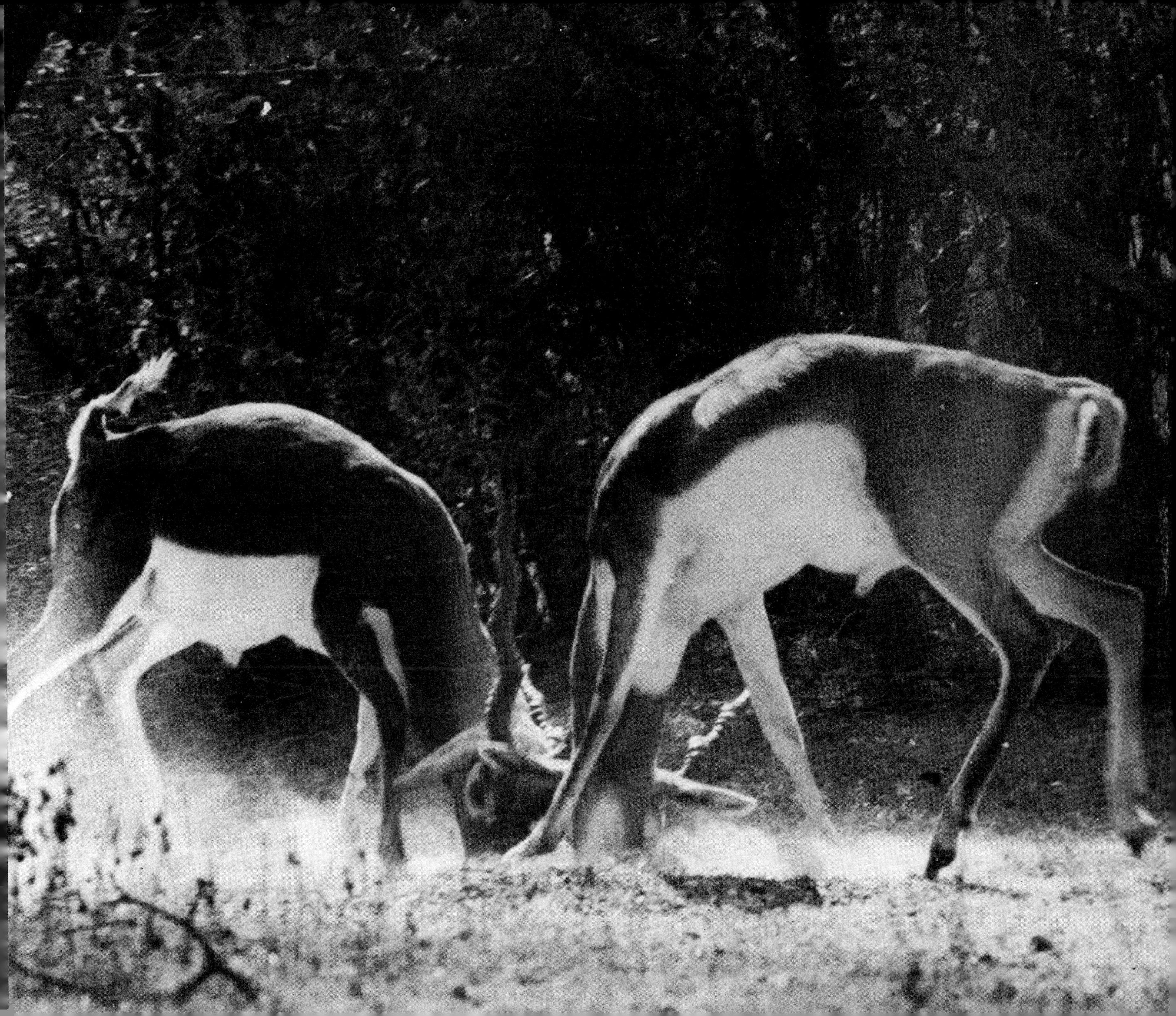

91 Sambar stag courting a doe
A rare picture so far not recorded. Photography of sambar is difficult as it lives in thick cover and comes out only after dark.

92 Courting stag
After battles are won the stag settles down to family life with a harem of two or three does. But he has to be constantly vigilant, to guard against intruders hovering around to snatch any doe in heat. Courtship takes place during the winter. The wound on the hind quarters of the stag was the fresh mark of a battle he had fought. Notice also the stag's rich winter coat.

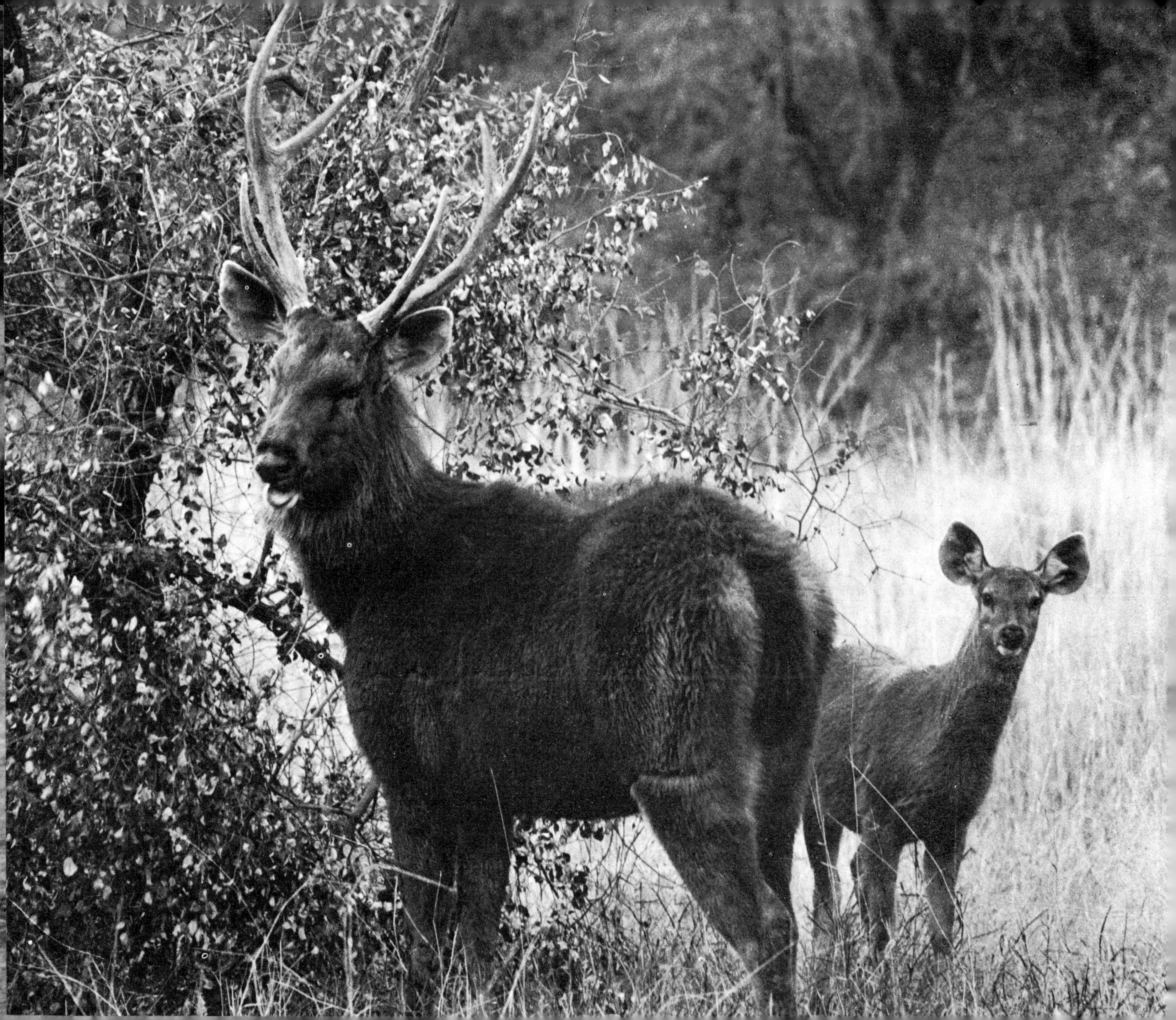

99 The scavengers
Jackals live in family units – father, mother and their young – and are found throughout Tigerland. They look for carrion, eggs, fruit and small rodents, as well as disabled or sick mammals and their young. Their movements are signalled by the lapwing's call.

100-2 Nature provides her own dustmen
Right and overleaf
The jackal is the principal of them. Here he disposes of the left-overs of a tiger's dinner – in collaboration with hyaenas, ratel, civets at night and vultures during the day. An abandoned kill is a feast for them, but no one dares approach until the tigers have finished.

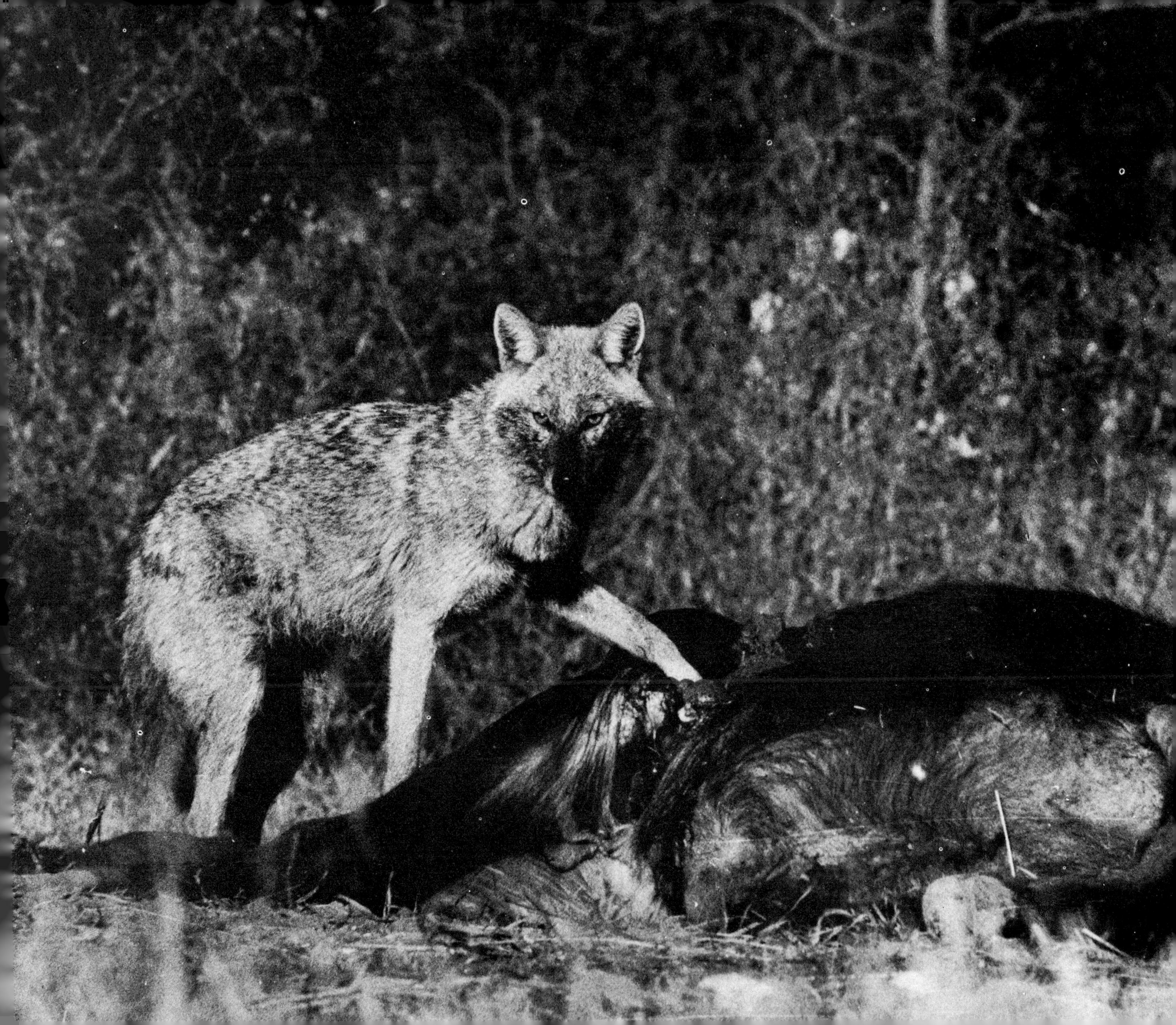

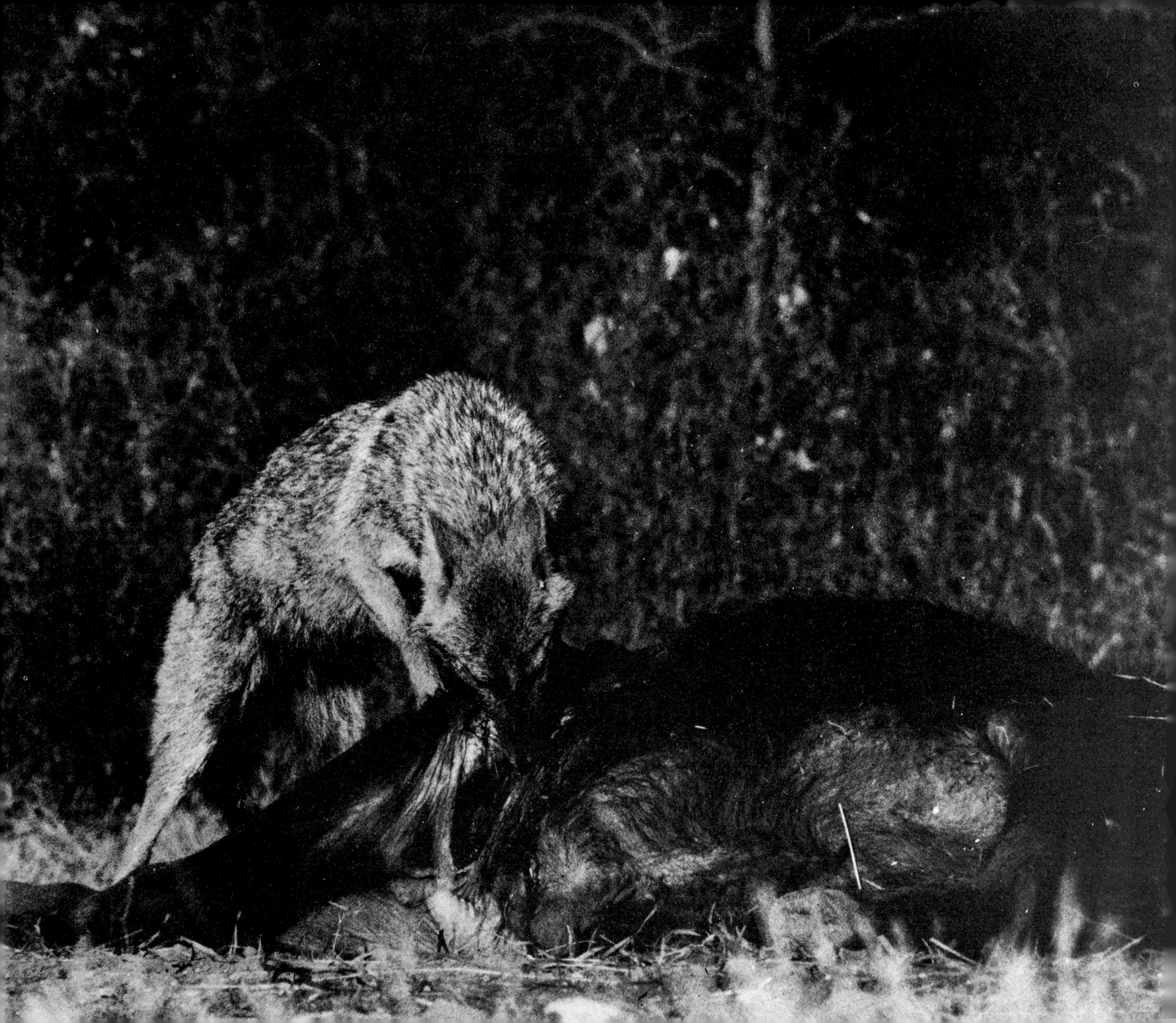

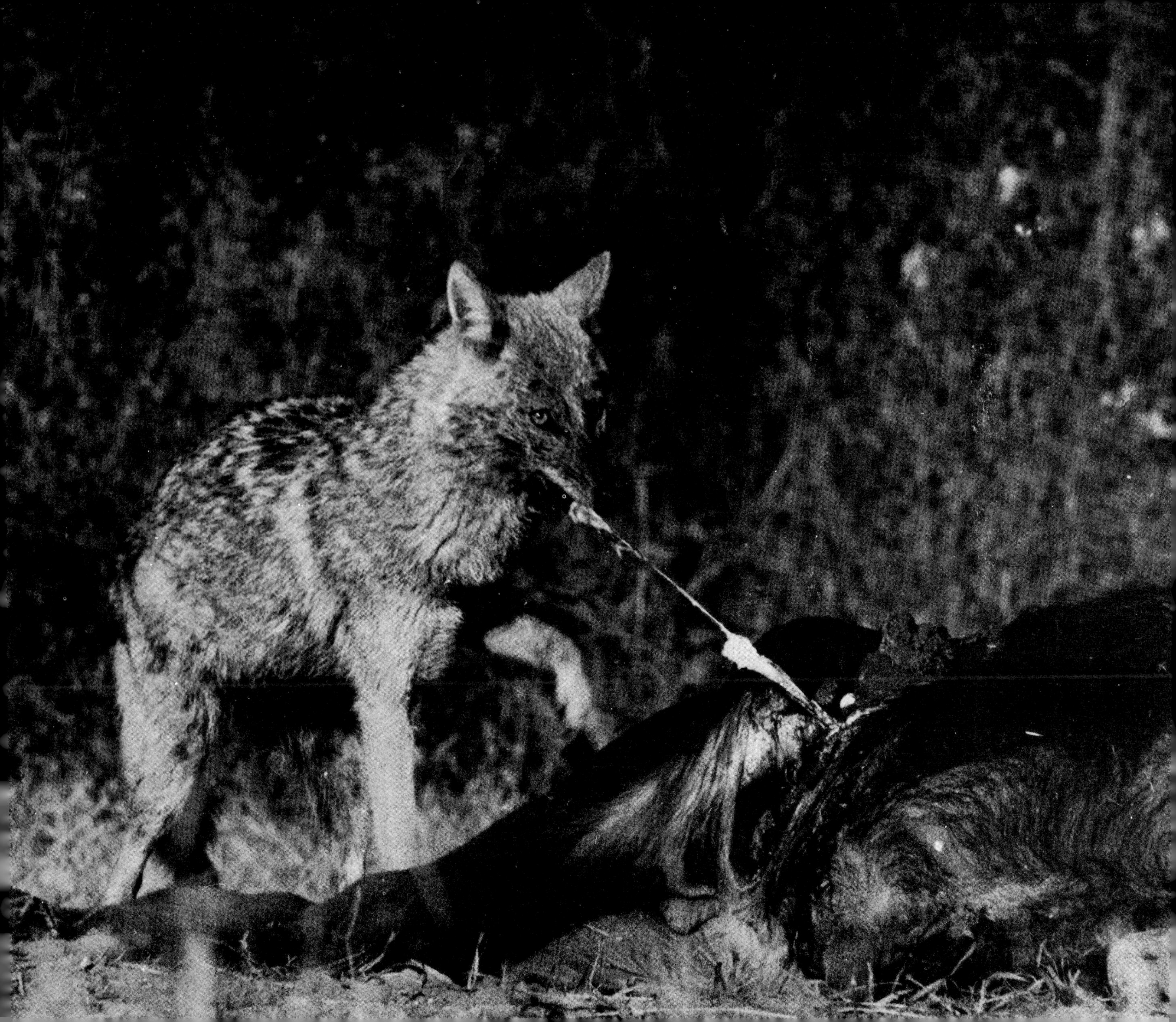

103 A soft landing
　　The vulture (*gyps benghalensis*) is breaking in its flight. Its neck is stretched, eyes focussed on the landing point and legs lowered, ready for touch down.

104 I saw it first!

This big bird, so often seen, is difficult to photograph because of light conditions. Being such a heavy bird, it has to take advantage of air currents to become airborne. These are available only during the hot hours of the day, a time unsuitable for photography. This picture was taken during the morning hours. The vultures discovered the carcass from their roosting tree and had only to descend for a meal.

The widespread wings and bent neck to scare any approaching bird lend excitement to the picture. They ended by sharing the meal.

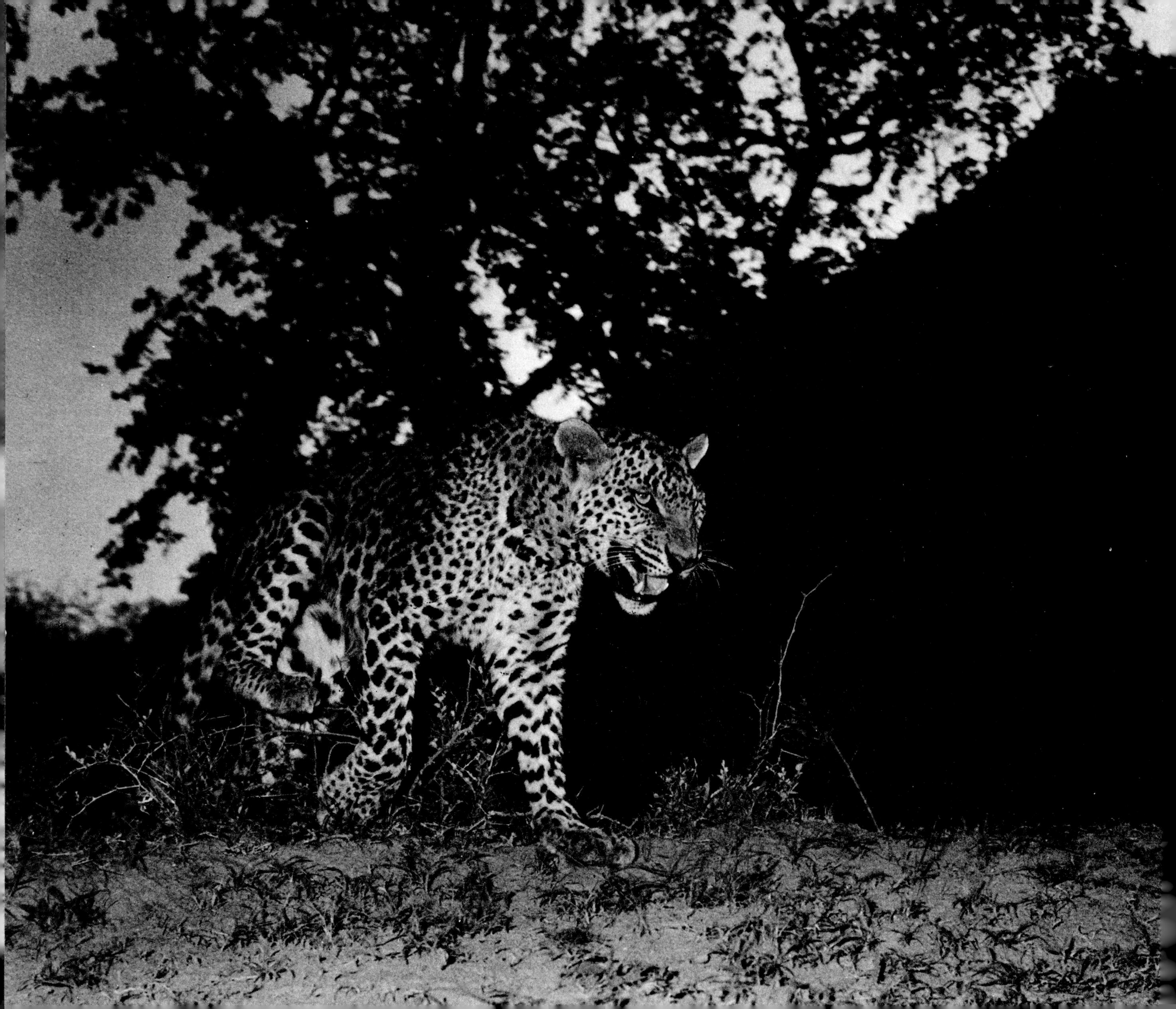

107 Prowling panther
The leopard is commonly called a panther. This one was intercepted by flashlight while moving towards his kill, partly eaten the previous night. The sun was down but the sky was still bright. The leopard's head stands out well against the dark shadow of the hillside. The leopard's habit of lifting either the two front or two hind legs simultaneously is amply demonstrated by this picture. The hind foot will be placed a little ahead of the forefoot, as in the case of lions and tigers.

108 A watchful gaze
Sambar stags are cautious, and will visit waterholes only late at night or before dawn, so as to avoid predators. I used a flashlight rather than a high light – hence the strangeness of the eyes – so I might catch the magnificence of the sambar's antlers.

111 A futile attempt
After killing its prey, a tiger will usually drag it out of the open and into safe cover. But if a carcass gets entangled the tiger is helpless, as he is unable to negotiate an obstacle. This tiger was one of the unlucky ones. When his kill got firmly caught up he simply gave one or two tugs at it, and left.

112 Myself as prey
With lowered head, elevated rump, straightened tail and eyes fixed on their target, this tiger is set for a quick rush. I was the object of his attention, hardly ten feet away.

113 Tyger, tyger, burning bright...
Overleaf
On this occasion, he intends no harm to his photographer. I took this picture from an open jeep at a distance of about 23 feet and in total darkness.

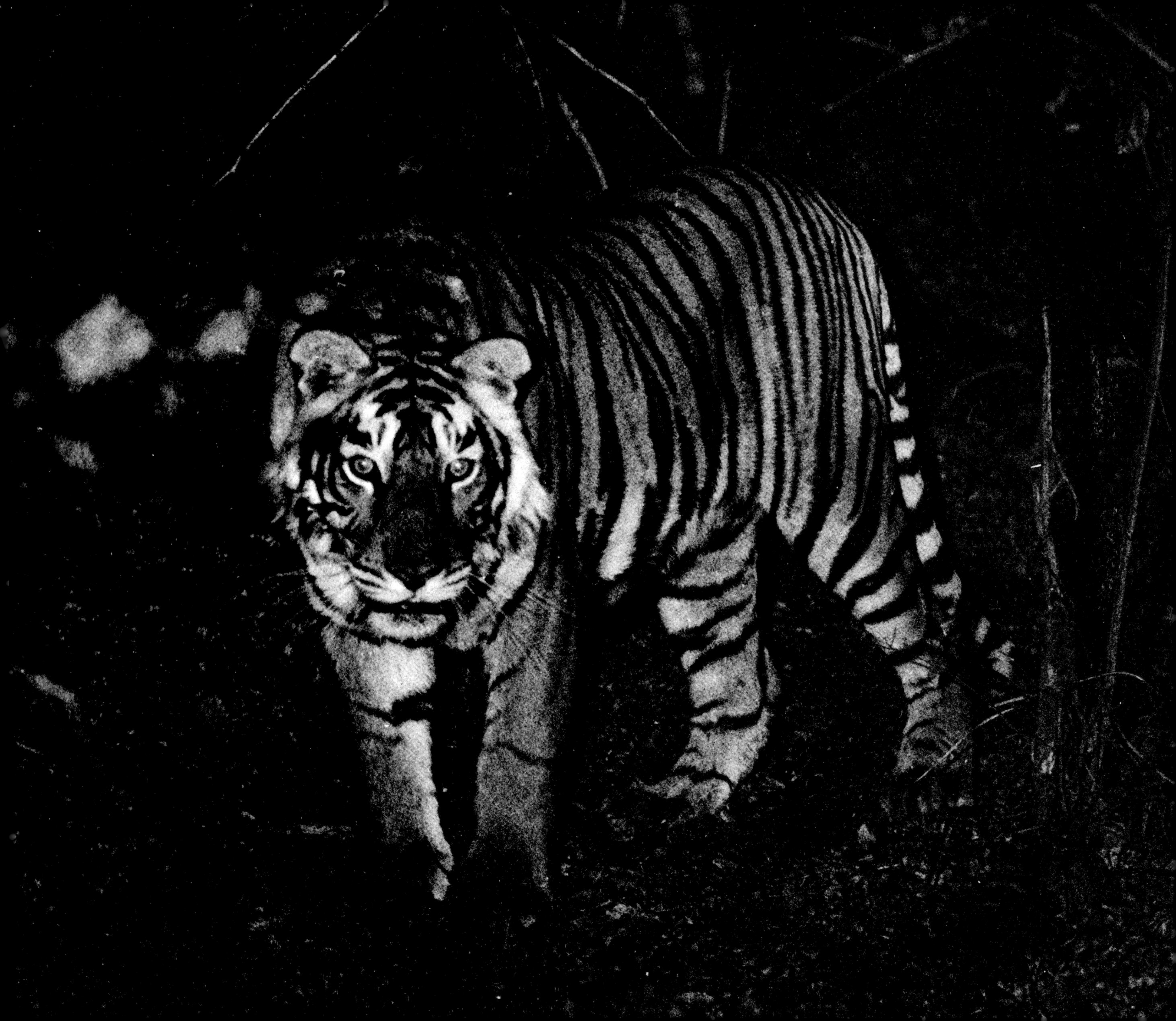

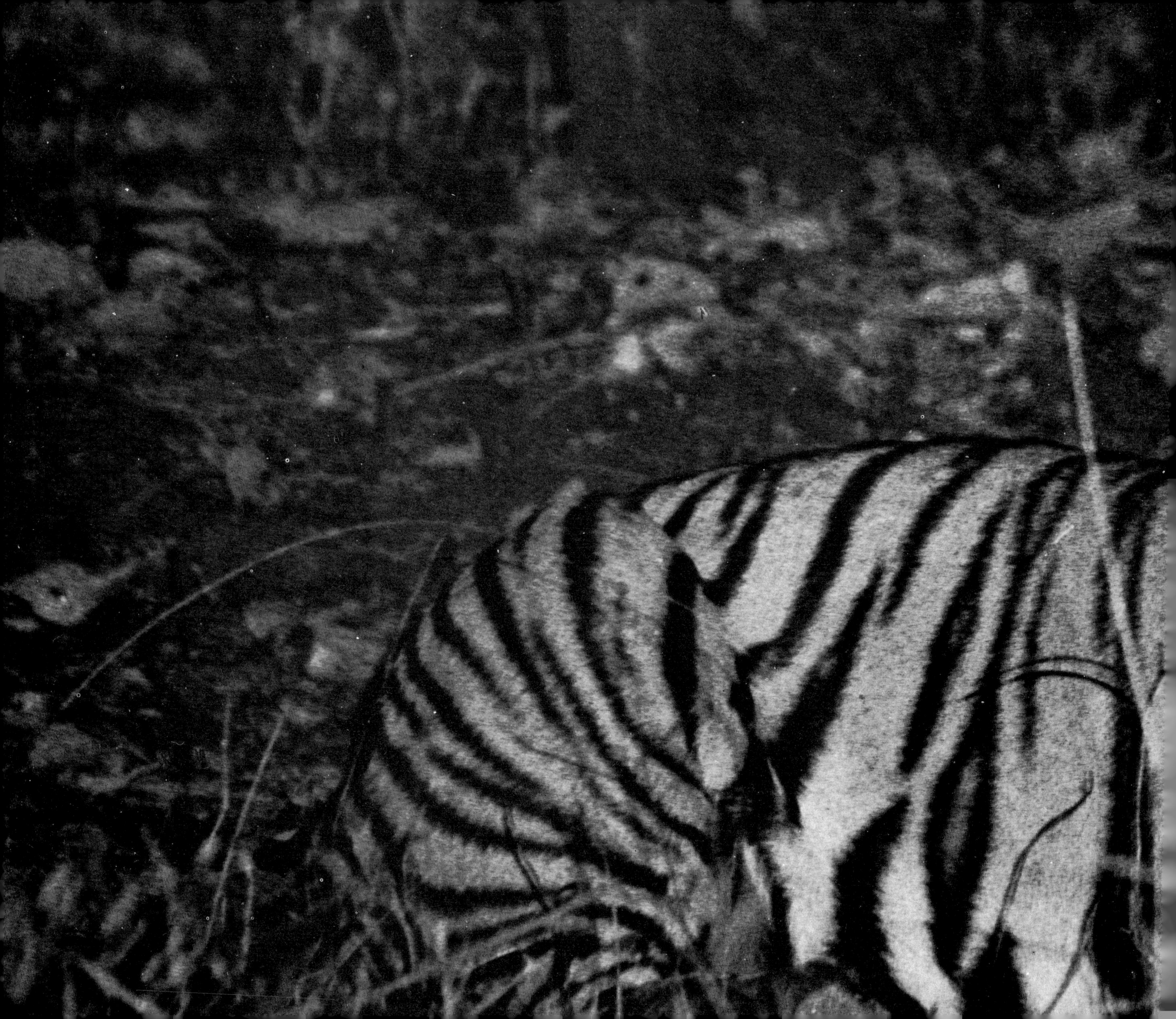

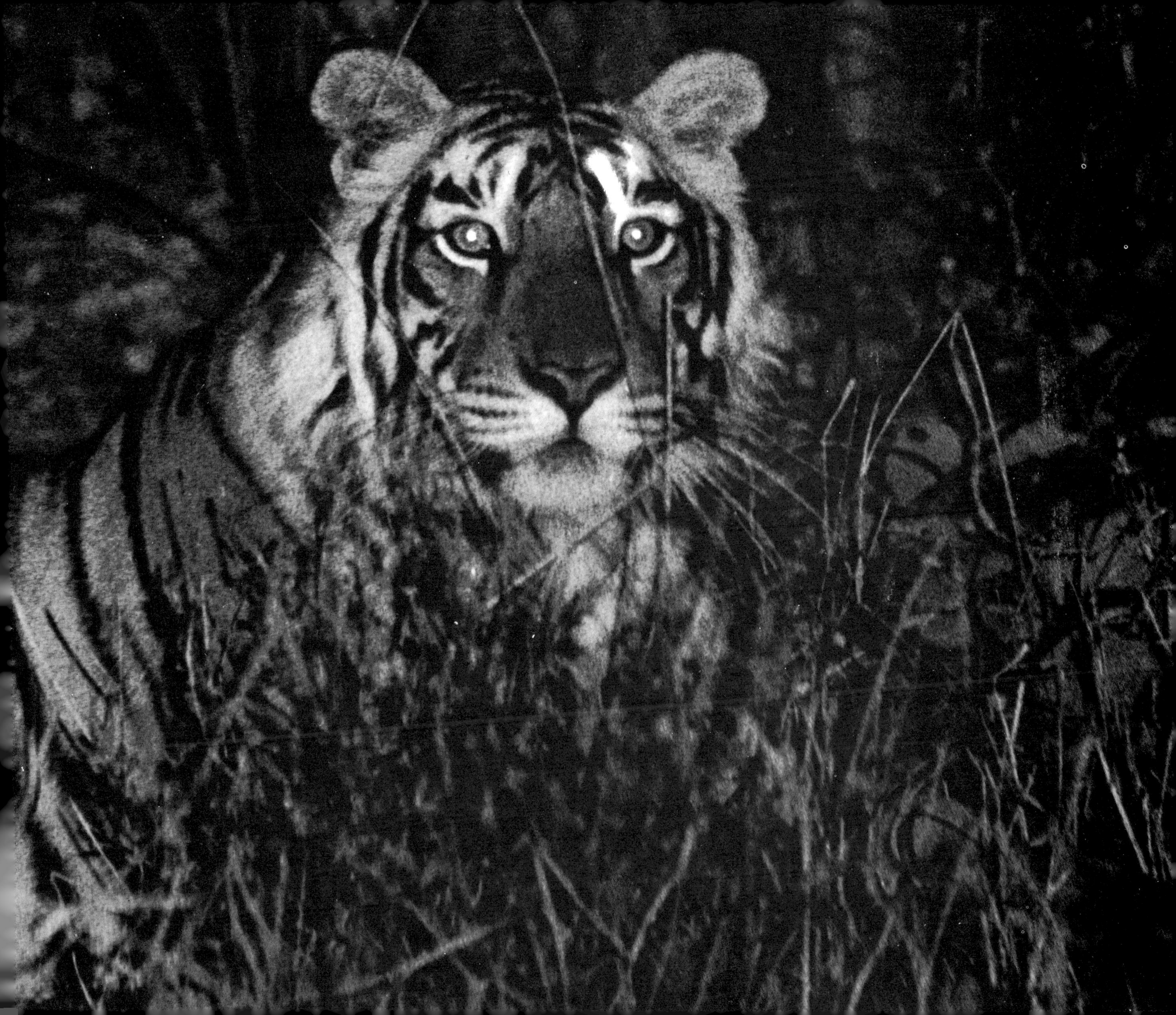

114 The banquet
They can hardly be called cubs though they are still under the care of their mother. But now she is allowing them freedom to explore and stalk. All of them struggle to get a better feeding position, and dinner is a noisy affair. My flashlight did not bother them, except for occasional glances. The picture was again taken in total darkness, so as to record their natural behaviour.

115 A successful search
Stalking tigers at night to get a good picture is a real challenge. Everything, from the discovery of a tiger to getting the correct focus and a successful flash, is an achievement.

116 Through the camera's eye *Overleaf*
This tiger was interrupted on his way to a waterhole. He sat down to watch my jeep, and calmly allowed me this close-up flashlit picture.

117 Shy but alert *Endpaper*
A fine picture of a tiger in a pool.

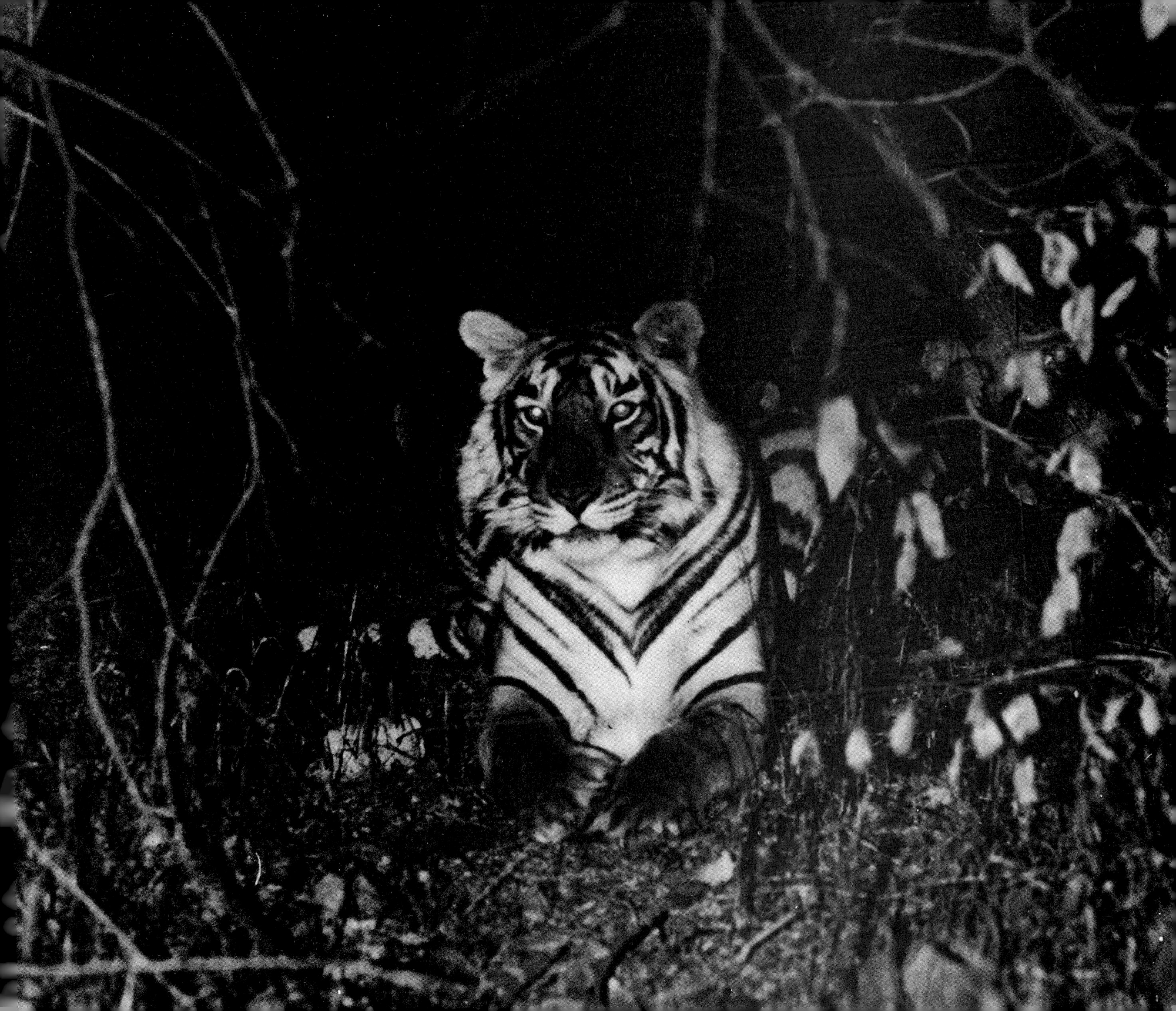

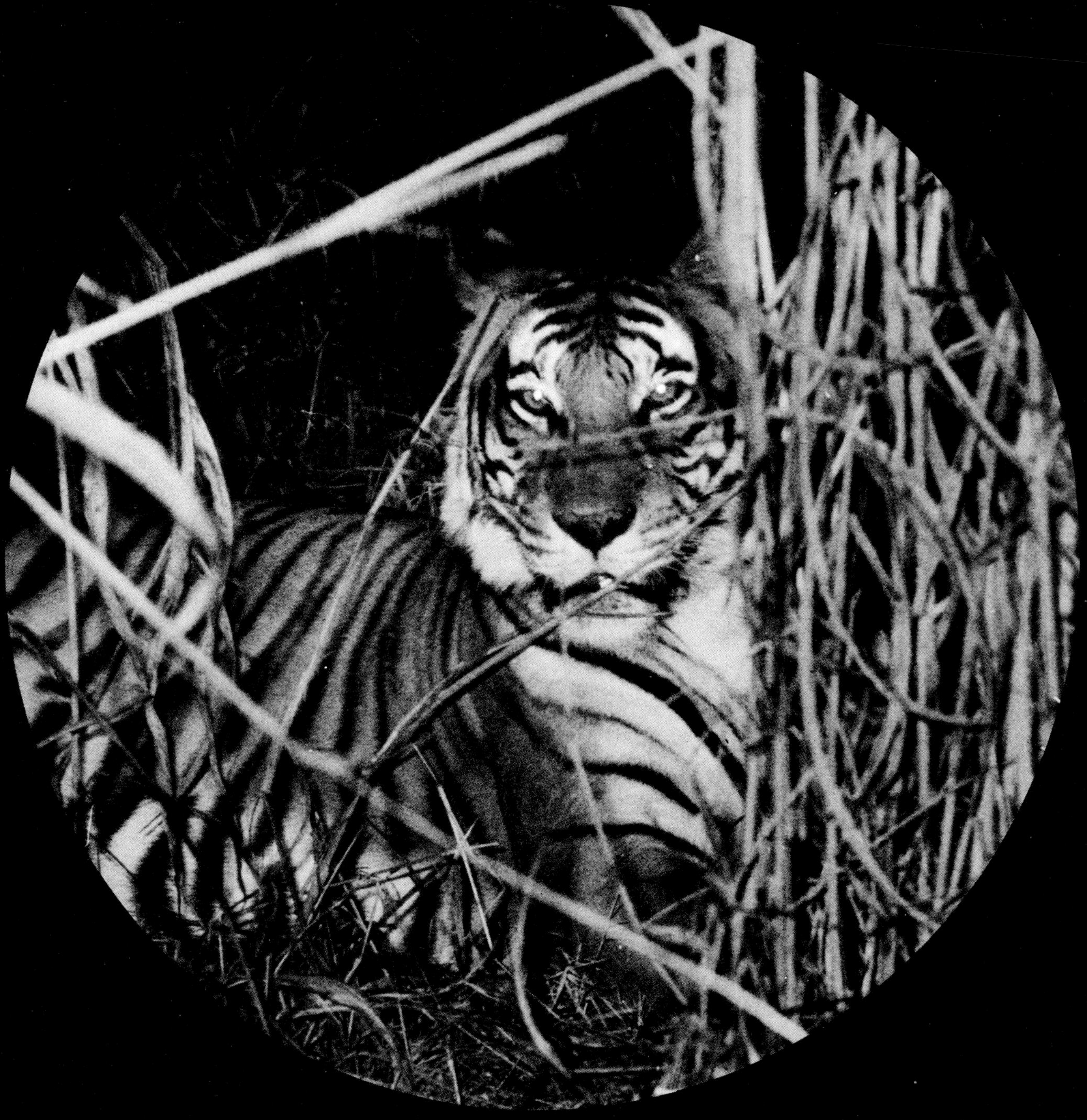